PRACTICAL ADVICE
TO TEACHERS

RUDOLF STEINER

PRACTICAL ADVICE
TO TEACHERS

Fourteen lectures given at the foundation
of the Waldorf School, Stuttgart, from
21 August to 5 September 1919

Translated by

JOHANNA COLLIS

RUDOLF STEINER PRESS
35 Park Road, London NW1 6XT

First published in English by Rudolf Steiner
Publishing Co., London, and Anthroposophic
Press, N.Y., 1937

Second Edition (new translation), Rudolf Steiner
Press, 1976

Translated from shorthand reports unrevised by the lec-
turer. The German text is published under the title:
Erziehungskunst. Methodisch-Didaktisches.(Vol. No. 294 in the
Bibliographical Survey, 1961).
  This English edition is published in agreement with the
Rudolf Steiner-Nachlassverwaltung, Dornach, Switzerland.

ISBN 0 85440 302 7 (cased)

0 85440 303 5 (paperback)

MADE AND PRINTED IN GREAT BRITAIN BY
THE GARDEN CITY PRESS LIMITED
LETCHWORTH, HERTFORDSHIRE, SG6 1JS

CONTENTS

EDITORIAL NOTE

Since Rudolf Steiner gave these lectures over fifty years ago to the first teachers of the first school to be established on principles suggested by him, there naturally occur references to the conditions in the general educational world that no longer exist or have never existed in English-speaking countries. Only in the most trivial sense do these references date the work. The depth of insight into the nature of the child, the combination of imagination and sheer common sense, give this 'practical advice' a universal quality. We may even be grateful that Rudolf Steiner did consider the practical difficulties that would be encountered in relation to state requirements or the social conditions of his time; teachers today are faced with similar pressures, though the details may be different. They may take courage and feel challenged by the passages which show just how certain obstacles can be encountered without undue sacrifice of educational ideals. Rudolf Steiner is concerned with the most effective and beneficial means of educating the child in whatever society he happens to live. The ideal is never divorced from the practical means of achieving it.

LECTURE ONE

Stuttgart, 21 August 1919

My dear friends,

We shall find it necessary in this course to distinguish between the lectures concerned with education in general and this group dealing more specifically with teaching methods. I should like also to say a few words by way of introduction, since in the actual methods it will be our task to use, we shall in all modesty have to differ from the methods that have arisen from quite other presuppositions than those on which our own are based. The methods we use will certainly not differ from those applied hitherto merely because we want to do something new or different out of obstinacy; they will be different because we shall have to recognize from the special tasks of our particular age how teaching must be done if mankind is in future to be able to fulfil the impulses of development prescribed by the universal cosmic order.

We shall above all have to realize that in employing our method we shall be dealing in a particular way with the harmonizing of the higher man, the man of spirit and soul, with the physical, bodily man, the lower man. The subjects you teach will not be treated in the way they have been dealt with hitherto. You will in a way have to use them as means with which to develop the soul and bodily forces of the individual in the right way. What matters for you will not be the transmitting of knowledge as such; you will be concerned with handling the knowledge for the purpose of developing human capacities. You will above all have to distinguish between subject matter which rests on convention or tradition (though this may not be clearly and concisely stated) and knowledge founded on a recognition of universal human nature.

When you teach a child reading and writing today, just consider quite externally the position of this reading and writing in our general cultural situation. We read, but the art of reading has evolved during the course of cultural development. The shapes of the letters that have arisen and the connections of the letter shapes with one another are purely a matter of convention. By teaching a child reading in its present form we are teaching him something that, apart from his place in a particular cultural period, has absolutely no significance for him as a human being. We must be aware that what we practise in the realm of physical culture has absolutely no direct significance for supra-physical mankind, for the supra-physical world. The belief put forward in certain circles, particularly among spiritualists, that the spirits use human script in order to bring it into the physical world, is quite erroneous. The writing used by human beings has arisen as a result of human activity and convention on the physical plane. The spirits are not in the least interested in complying with these physical conventions. Even if it is a fact that the spirits do communicate with us, they do so only through the mediumship of a human being who fulfils a translating function; the spirits do not directly of themselves transform what lives in them into a form which can be written and read. The reading and writing you teach the child rests on convention; it is something that has arisen within life on the physical plane.

Teaching the child arithmetic is quite another matter. You will sense that here the most important thing is not the shapes of the figures but the reality that lives in these shapes. This living reality has much more meaning for the spiritual world than that which lives in reading and writing. Finally, if we even embark on teaching the child certain activities which we may call artistic, we enter the sphere that quite definitely has eternal meaning, that reaches up into the activity of the spirit and soul in man. In teaching children reading and writing we are working in the most exclusively physical domain; in arithmetic our teaching is already less physical; and in music or drawing or kindred fields we really teach the soul-spirit or spirit-soul of the child.

Now in a rationally conducted lesson we can combine these three impulses of the supra-physical in artistic activity, the partly supra-physical in arithmetic and the totally physical in reading and writing, thus bringing about a harmonizing of the human being. Imagine for example (today I am only introducing the subject and shall just touch aphoristically on certain points) approaching the child by saying: You have seen a fish, haven't you? Try and remember what the fish looked like when you saw it. If I do this on the blackboard (see left sketch) it looks very like a fish, doesn't it? The fish you saw looked rather like this drawing on the blackboard. Now imagine you wanted to say *fish*. What you say when you say *fish* lies in this sign (see left sketch). Now try not to say *fish* but only to start saying it.— Now we try to teach the child only to start saying *fish*, f-f-f-: There now you see, you have started to say *fish*. Now suppose people in olden times gradually started to make this sign simpler (see right sketch). When you start to say

fish, f-f-f-, you express it in writing by making just this sign. And now people call this sign F. So you have learnt that what you express when you say *fish* starts with F, and now you write it down as F. Whenever you start writing *fish* you breathe f-f-f with your breath. So you learn the sign for when you start to say *fish*!—

When you start appealing to the nature of the child in this way you really transport him back to earlier cultural ages, for this is how writing originally arose. Later the process became a mere convention so that today we no longer recognize the connection between the abstract letter shapes and the pictures that arose purely out of seeing things and imitating what was seen in the form of drawings. All the letters have arisen out of such picture shapes. And now think how if you teach the child only the convention: This is how you make an F!—you are teaching him something purely derivative and disconnected from the human context. Writing is then divorced from the medium in which it arose, the artistic medium. That is why when we teach writing we must start with the artistic drawing of the forms, the forms of the consonants, if we want to reach back far enough for the child to be moved by the differences of the forms. It is not enough just to tell the child by word of mouth; this is the very thing that has made people what they are today. By lifting the shapes of letters out of today's conventions and showing the source from which they have emerged, we move the whole being of the child and make something quite different of him than would be the case were we simply to appeal to his intellect. We must not allow ourselves to think only in abstracts. We must teach art in drawing and so on, we must teach soul substance in arithmetic, and we must teach the conventional artistically in reading and writing: we must permeate the whole of our teaching with an artistic element. From the very beginning we shall therefore have to set great store by fostering what is artistic in the child. The artistic element works particularly strongly on the will nature of man. In this way we can penetrate to something that is connected with man's whole being, whereas whatever is linked to the conventional has something to do only with the head sphere of man. So we shall proceed in such a way that every child is enabled to draw and paint. Thus we start in the simplest fashion with drawing and drawing-painting. From the start we shall also foster music so that the child becomes accustomed right away to handling a musical instrument; in this way, too, the child's artistic feeling is quickened. Then he will also learn to sense in his whole being something that is otherwise only conventional.

It will be our task to find teaching methods that all the time engage the whole human being. We should not succeed in this were we not to turn our attention to developing the latent artistic sense of the human being. In bringing about this development we strengthen the individual's inclination later to find an interest in the whole world in keeping with his total being. The fundamental flaw hitherto has always been that people have stood in the world with their head nature only, merely trailing the rest of their being along behind. The consequence is that these other parts of man's being are now guided by their animal urges, indulging in untamed emotions—such as we are just experiencing in what is spreading so curiously from the Eastern part of Europe. Such a phenomenon has arisen because the being of man has not been fostered in its totality. It is not just that the artistic element must be cultivated; the actual teaching of every lesson must be drawn from the artistic realm. Every method must be immersed in the artistic element. Educating and teaching must become a real art. Subject matter must not be more than the underlying basis.

So from the sphere of drawing we shall derive first the written forms of the letters and then the printed forms. On the basis of drawing we shall build up reading. You will see that in this way we strike a chord with which the childish soul will happily vibrate in unison because the child then has not only an external interest; he sees for instance how a sound he breathes finds expression in reading and writing.

Then we shall have to rearrange a great deal in our teaching. You will see that what we today aim at in reading and writing can of course not be built up exclusively in the manner indicated here; all we shall be able to do is awaken the forces necessary for such a building-up. For if, with life being what it is today, we were to build up our teaching on the process of evolving reading and writing from drawing, we would have to keep the children at school till they were twenty; the usual schooling period would not be long enough. All we can do now is carry out the method in principle while still proceeding to educate the children, always remaining in the artistic element. After working through individual letters in this way for a while we shall then have to go on to make the child understand that grown-up people can discover a meaning in these curious shapes. While cultivating further what the child has learnt like this from isolated instances, we pass on (no matter whether the child understands the details or not) to writing whole sentences. In these sentences the child will notice shapes, for instance the F he has become familiar with in *fish*. He will notice other shapes besides, which through lack of time cannot be dealt with individually. The next step will be to write the different printed letters on the blackboard and then one day we put a whole long sentence on the board and say to the child: This is what grown-up people have in front of them when they have formed out everything in the way we formed out the F in *fish* and so on.—Then we teach the child to copy down the writing. We shall make sure that what he sees passes over into his hands so that he not only reads with his eyes but also forms what he reads with his hands; in this way he will know that he can himself form whatever may be on the blackboard. We shall not let the child learn to read without being able to form with his hand what he sees, both handwriting and the printed letters. In this way we shall achieve something of utmost importance: that the child never reads with his eyes only but that in a mysterious way the activity of the eyes passes over into his whole limb activity. The children then feel unconsciously right down into their legs what they would otherwise only pass over with their eyes. It is our aim to interest the whole human being in this activity.

After this we may reverse the procedure. We split up the sentence we have written down and by atomizing the words we show the forms of the other letters we have not yet derived from their elements; we proceed from the whole to the parts. For instance if we have written the word KOPF (head) the child learns to write KOPF just by copying it down. Then we split the words into its separate letters: K, O, P, F; we go from the whole to the parts.

This sequence of starting from the whole and proceeding to the parts must in fact be present in everything we teach. On another occasion we might take a piece of paper and cut it into a number of pieces. Then we count the pieces; let us say there are 24. We say to the child: Look, I describe these pieces of paper I have cut by what I have written down here, 24 pieces of paper. (It could just as well be beans.) Now watch carefully. I take some of the pieces of paper away and make another little heap with them; then I make a third and fourth heap. I have made four little heaps out of the 24 pieces of paper. Now I shall count the pieces; you cannot do that yet, but I can. The pieces in the first heap I shall call 'nine', those in the second 'five', those in the third 'seven', and those in the fourth 'three'. You see: first I had one single heap, 24 pieces of paper; now I have four heaps, 9, 5, 7 and 3 pieces of paper. It is all the same paper. If I have it all together I call it 24; and if I have it in four little heaps I call it 9, 5, 7 and 3 pieces of paper. And now I can say that 24 pieces of paper are 9, 5, 7 and 3 pieces together.—In this way I have taught the child to add up. I did not start with the separate addenda from which a sum total could be derived. This would be quite out of keeping with man's original nature. (Please refer to my book *A Theory of Knowledge based on Goethe's World Conception.*[1]) It is the reverse procedure which is in keeping with human nature: first the sum total is considered and this is then divided into the separate addenda. So we teach the child adding up by reversing the usual procedure: we start with the sum and then proceed to the addenda. The child will grasp the concept of 'together' much better as a result than if we were to pick the addenda first and then lump them together in the usual fashion. Our teaching methods will have to differ from the usual by teaching the child as it were the opposite way round what a sum total is in contrast to the separate addenda. We shall then also be able to expect quite a different understanding from the child than would be possible with the reverse procedure. You will only be able to discover what is most important about this through practical experience. You will notice how the child enters into the subject in quite a different way with quite a different capacity to absorb what is taught if you start out in the manner described.

You can then apply the opposite process for the next step in arithmetic. You say: Now I shall put all the pieces of paper together again. Then I take some away, making two heaps. And I call the heap I have taken away 'three'. How have I come by this 3? By taking it away from the others. When they were together I called it 24; now I have taken 3 away and call the remainder 21.—In this way you proceed to the concept of subtraction. That is to say once again you start not from the minuend and subtrahend but from the remainder that is left over, and you lead from this to what the remainder came from. Here you tread the reverse path. And thus you can extend to the whole art of arithmetic this method of going always from the whole to the parts, as you will see later when we come to the methods used for special subjects. There is nothing for it in this connection but to accustom ourselves to a teaching process quite different from the one we are used to. We proceed in a manner which fosters not only the subject matter we are imparting (which must of course not be neglected, though it is today given rather disproportionate attention) but at the same time the child's sense for authority. We say continually: I call this 24, I call this 9.—When I stress in the anthroposophical lectures that the sense for authority must be fostered between the ages of seven and fourteen I do not mean that the children must be drilled into a feeling for authority. The necessary element can flow from the very technique of teaching. It reigns as an undertone. The child listens and says: Ah, so he calls that 9, he calls that 24, and so on.—The child obeys spontaneously. By listening to the person teaching in this way, he is permeated with what is to emerge as the sense for authority. This is the secret. Any artificial drilling of the sense for authority should be excluded by the very nature of the method.

Next we must be fully aware that we always want to bring about the working together of willing, feeling and thinking. If we teach in this way, willing, feeling and thinking do indeed work together. It is a matter of never pointing the will in the wrong direction by false means; instead the strengthening of the will must be brought to proper expression by the use of artistic means. This purpose is served from the start by artistic painting and also musical instruction. You will notice that early on in the second period of his life the child is most receptive to authoritative teaching by means of the artistic and that most can therefore be achieved with him then by this means. He will quite effortlessly find his way into what we want to convey to him and will take the utmost delight in putting some of it down on paper in drawing or even painting; we have only to see to it that mere external copying is avoided. Here too we shall have to remind ourselves that we must in a way transport the child back into earlier ages, though we cannot proceed as though we were still in those ages. People were simply different then. Nowadays you will transport the child back to these earlier cultural ages with quite a different disposition of soul and spirit. This is why in drawing we

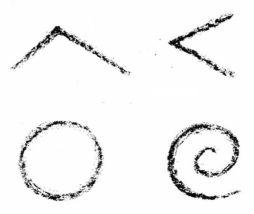

shall not be aiming at making the child copy this or that; we shall teach him archetypal forms in drawing, showing him how to make one angle like this and another like that; we shall endeavour to reveal to him the circle and the spiral. Our point of departure will be the form as such, irrespective of whether it imitates this or that; we shall endeavour to awaken the child's interest in the form itself. Perhaps you recall the lecture in which I attempted to awaken a feeling for the development of the acanthus leaf.[2] I explained that it is entirely false to suppose that the leaf of the acanthus plant was copied in the form in which it appears in legend; the acanthus leaf simply arose out of an inner formative impulse and only subsequently was it felt: this resembles nature. So it was not a question of copying nature. We shall have to take this into account in the realm of drawing and painting. Then at last there will be an end to the frightful error that so desolates the minds of men. Whenever they meet something man-made they say: This is natural, this is unnatural.— It is totally irrelevant to judge whether something is copied properly and so on. A resemblance to the external should appear only as something secondary. What should live in man is his inner closeness to the forms themselves. Thus even if we draw a nose we must have an inner relationship to the shape of a nose so that only subsequently does the resemblance of the shape to a nose become obvious. Between the ages of seven and fourteen a sense for the inner law of things can never be awakened by means of external copying. We must realize: What can be developed between the ages of seven and fourteen can no longer be developed at a later stage. The forces at work during that period die away; later all that can arise is a substitute, unless an individual undergoes a complete transformation of the kind called an initiation, either naturally or unnaturally.

I am now going to say something unusual, but we must refer back to the principles of human nature if we want to be teachers in the true sense today. There are exceptional cases in which an individual can recover a certain amount later in life. But then he must have been through a severe illness or suffered some other kind of deformity, for instance have broken a leg which was then not set properly; in other words he must have undergone a certain loosening of the etheric body from the physical body. This is of course a dangerous matter. If it comes about as a result of karma we have to accept it. But it cannot be counted upon; nor can there be any regulations in public life stipulating that a person may catch up in this way on something thus missed, to say nothing of other things. The development of the human being is a mysterious matter, and in all that we strive for in teaching and education we should never reckon with the abnormal but always with the normal. Thus teaching is always a social matter. Therefore account must constantly be taken of the proper age at which to develop specific forces so that their cultivation may enable the individual to take his place in life in the right way. We have to reckon with the fact that certain capacities can only be unfolded between the seventh and fourteenth years in a way that will enable the individual to cope with life later on. If these capacities are not developed during this period, people are unable to cope with life's battles later, as is indeed the case with most people today.

The ability to take their place artistically in this way in the workings of the world is what we as teachers have to bestow on the children we educate. Man's nature, we shall find, is such that he is in a way a born musician. If people were sufficiently agile they would dance with all little children, they would move in some way with all little children. Man is born into the world in a way that makes him want to join his own bodily nature in a musical rhythm and relationship with the world; and this inner musical capacity is most strongly present in children in their third and fourth years. Parents could do a tremendous amount, if they would only notice this, by starting not so much from external musicality but from the attunement of the physical body and from the element of the dance. Just in this period of life infinitely much could be gained by permeating the little child's body with elementary eurythmy. If the parents would learn to do eurythmy with their children, something quite different would arise in them than is usually the case. They would overcome a certain heaviness that lives in the limbs. Everybody has this heaviness in the limbs nowadays;

and this would be overcome. At the change of teeth there would then remain in the child the foundation for the whole musical element. It is from this musical element that the separate senses arise: the musically attuned ear, the eye for shapes and forms. The musically attuned ear and the eye appreciative of line and form are specializations of the total musical human being. Thus we must definitely cherish the idea that in drawing on the artistic element we assimilate into the upper man, the nerve-sense man, the disposition of the entire being. By means of music or by means of drawing or modelling, we lift the realm of feeling up into the intellectual sphere. This must happen in the right way. Today everything is blurred and mixed, especially when the artistic is cultivated. We draw with our hands, and we model with our hands, yet the two activities are totally different. This is expressed particularly clearly when we introduce children to the artistic realm. When we guide children into the realm of what can be modelled, we must as far as possible see to it that they follow the plastic forms with their hands. By feeling the way he makes his own forms, by moving his hand and making a drawing, the child can be brought to follow the forms with his eyes but also with his will emerging through his eyes. It is no violation of the child's naivety if we teach him to follow the forms of the body with the hollow of his hand or if we make him aware of his eyes, for instance by letting him follow a complete circle with his eyes and then saying: You are making a circle with your eyes.—This does not wound the child's naivety; it engages the interest of the whole human being. We must therefore be aware that we lift the lower part of the human being up into the higher part, the nerve-sense being.

In this way we shall gain a certain feeling that becomes the foundation of our method, a feeling we have to cultivate in ourselves as educators and teachers that cannot directly

be imparted to anyone else. Suppose we have before us a
human being whom we are to teach and educate, that is to
say: a child. The perception of the growing human being is
vanishing today as far as education is concerned; everything
is confused. We must grow accustomed to differentiating in
the way we regard this child. We must in a certain way
accompany the teaching and educating we do with inner
sensations, inner feelings, and also inner stirrings of the will
which vibrate as in a lower octave without being acted out.
We must be aware: In the growing child the ego and the
astral body gradually develop; through heredity the etheric
and the physical body are already present. It is good if we
now think to ourselves: The physical body and the etheric
body are always particularly cultivated from the head
downwards. The head rays out what actually creates the
physical man. If we conduct the proper educational and
teaching procedures with the head, we are serving the
growth organization in the best possible way. If we teach
the child in a way that draws the head element out of the
whole being, then what is right moves from the head to the
limbs: the person grows better, learns to walk better, and so
on. We can therefore say: If we develop in the appropriate
way all that has to do with the upper man, the physical and
the etheric will stream downwards. If we have the feeling,
when we teach reading and writing in a more intellectual
way, that the child is open to us when he takes in what we
offer him, we shall send this out from the head into the rest
of the body. Ego and astral body, on the other hand, are
formed from below upwards if the whole human being is
encompassed by education. A strong feeling of ego would
arise, for instance, if we were to offer the child elementary
eurythmy between his third and fourth year. This would
make a claim on the whole individual and a proper ego
feeling would strike root in his being. If we furthermore tell
him many things that give him joy and others that cause

him pain, this forms the astral body from the lower being upwards. Just reflect for a moment a little more intimately on your own experiences. I expect you will all have had this experience: Walking along the street you were startled by something; you found that not only your head and your heart were shocked but also your limbs in which the feeling of shock lingered on. You will conclude from this that surrendering to something which releases feelings and excitement affects the whole human being, not just heart and head.

This is a truth that the educator and teacher must have very clearly in mind. He must see to it that the whole being of the child is moved. Consider from this point of view the telling of legends and fairy tales; if you have the right feeling for these and are thus able to tell them out of your own mood, you will tell them in a way that enables the children to feel with their whole body something of what is told. You are then really addressing yourself to the astral body of the child. Something rays up from the astral body into the head which the child ought to feel there. You should sense that you are gripping the whole child and that it is from the feelings and excitement you arouse that an understanding comes to the child of what you are telling. You may therefore consider it ideal, when you are telling the child legends or fairy tales or while you draw or paint with him, that you do not explain anything or work with concepts but seek to move the child's whole being so that when he then leaves you he only later out of himself reaches an understanding of what you have told. Try therefore to educate the ego and the astral body from below upwards in such a way that the head and heart follow later. Try not to tell the stories in a way that causes them to be reflected in the head and understanding; tell them in a way that evokes a kind of silent thrilled awe—within limits—and also pleasures and sorrows which echo on when the child has left you and only after a while are transformed into understanding and interest. Try to let your influence arise out of your close intimacy with the children. Try not to arouse interest artificially by counting on sensationalism; attempt rather to achieve an inner connection with the children and then let interest arise out of their own being.

How can this be done with a whole class? With a single child it is relatively easy. So long as you are fond of the child and seek only in love to do things with him you will find that his whole being is reached and not only his heart and head. And it is no more difficult with a whole class if you yourself are moved by the things you tell or do and are not only interested with your heart and head. Take a simple example: I want to make clear to the child the continued life of the soul after death. I shall only be deceiving myself and never make it clear to him if I merely teach him theories on the subject. No kind of concept can teach a child under the age of fourteen anything about immortality. I can, however, say to him: See this chrysalis; it is empty. Once there was a butterfly inside, but it has crept out.—I can also show him the process when it happens. It is good to demonstrate such metamorphoses to the child. Then I can make the comparison: Imagine you yourself are a chrysalis like this. Your soul is in you; later it will emerge just as the butterfly emerges from the chrysalis.—This is, of course, rather naively put. Now you can talk about this for a long time, but if you yourself do not believe that the butterfly is a picture of the human soul you will not achieve much with the child when you use the comparison. You ought not to allow yourself that utter untruth of seeing the whole idea merely as a made-up comparison. It is not just a made-up comparison but a fact placed before us by the divine world order. The two things are not just invented by our intellect. And if our attitude to such things is right, we learn to believe in the fact that nature everywhere offers us comparisons for actualities in the realm of soul and spirit. When we become one with what we teach the child, then the way we work affects the whole child. Being no longer able to feel with the child but believing instead in merely transposing everything into a rationality we ourselves do not believe in, this is the cause of our teaching the child so little. Through our own comprehension our relationship with the facts must be such that in the image, for instance, of the butterfly emerging from the chrysalis we bring to the child's soul not just an arbitrary picture but an example we ourselves understand and believe in, given by the divine world powers. The child must understand not merely through his ears; communication must be from soul to soul. If you take note of this you will make progress.

LECTURE TWO

Stuttgart, 22 August 1919

We shall now set about developing further what we outlined yesterday. You will have seen from what was said that even in the details of teaching methods a great deal will have to be transformed and renewed.

Consider for a moment what I brought to your notice an hour ago.[3] If you examine what I put before you, you will find that you can regard man as a being bearing within him three focal points in each of which sympathy and antipathy meet. Thus we can say that antipathy and sympathy meet even in the head. We can simply schematically state: Let us assume that in a certain part of the head the nervous system is interrupted for the first time, the sense perceptions enter and are met by antipathy coming from the human being.— From an example like this you can see that you must think of each individual system again in the whole human being, for sense activity as such is really a delicate limb activity taking place in such a way that sympathy holds sway in the sense sphere while antipathy is sent to meet it by the nervous system. So taking the activity of seeing, you will find that a kind of sympathy comes about in the eye—the blood vessels of the eye; and antipathy streams through this sympathy—the nervous system of the eye. In this way seeing comes about.

Now there is a second, for us at this moment more important, meeting between sympathy and antipathy in the central part of man. There sympathy and antipathy also meet, so that in man's middle system, his chest system, we again have a meeting of sympathy and antipathy. Again the whole human being is active, for when sympathy and antipathy meet in our middle system we are aware of this. You know also that this meeting can be expressed in our reaction to an impression with a rapid reflex action in which we do not think very much because we simply take evasive action, quite instinctively, against something threatening danger. Such more subconscious reflex actions are then also mirrored in the brain, in the soul, and in this way the whole acquires again a kind of pictorial character. We accompany with pictures what takes place in our chest organization as regards the meeting between sympathy and antipathy. Something takes place in the breast which is extraordinarily closely connected with the whole life of the human being. A meeting between sympathy and antipathy takes place that is connected in an extraordinarily significant way with our external life.

We develop in our whole being a certain activity that works as sympathy, an activity of sympathy. And we make this sympathetic activity interact continually in our chest organization with a cosmic activity of antipathy. The expression of these sympathetic and antipathetic activities that meet in this way is the speech of human beings. And a clear accompaniment by the brain to this meeting of sympathy and antipathy in the breast is the understanding of speech. We follow speech with understanding. In speech there is fundamentally an activity that takes place in the breast and a parallel activity that takes place in the head; but in the breast this activity is far more real while in the head it fades into an image. When you speak you actually have constantly the breast activity which you accompany with an image, the head activity. You will easily see from this that speaking rests basically on a constant rhythm of sympathetic and antipathetic activity, as does feeling. Speech is indeed in the first instance rooted in feeling. The fact that for speech we have the content that is identical with thoughts stems from the way we accompany the feeling content with the knowledge content, the picture content. We shall, however, only be able to understand the phenomenon of speech if we really conceive of it as being rooted in human feeling.

Speech is, in fact, doubly rooted in human feeling. First it is rooted in all that the human being brings towards the world in his feeling life. What is it that man brings to the world in his feelings? Let us take a distinct feeling, a distinct nuance of feeling, for instance astonishment, amazement. So long as we remain within the human being, within this microcosm, with our soul, we have to do with amazement or astonishment. But if we are enabled to establish a cosmic connection, a cosmic relationship that can be connected with this feeling nuance of amazement, then amazement turns into the sound 'O'.* The sound 'O' is really nothing other than the breath working in us when it is seized inwardly by amazement, by astonishment. You can therefore regard the 'O' sound as the expression of amazement, astonishment.

In the external consideration of the world in recent times speech has always been linked to something external. The question asked was: What is the origin of the link between the sounds and what they signify? But nobody realized that everything in the world makes an impression on the feelings of the individual. In some cases this may be so faint that it remains half unconscious. But we shall never find anything which we describe with a word containing the sound 'O' that does not in some way engender astonishment, however slight. If you say 'Ofen' (oven, stove), you are saying a word that contains an 'O' sound because something is inherent in it which causes some slight astonishment. In this

* Translator's note: The vowels discussed in this lecture are the pure vowel sounds of the original German: 'A' as in father, 'E' as in eight, 'I' as in me, 'O' as in order, 'U' as in moon.

way speech is rooted in human feelings. In feelings you are linked to the whole world and you give the whole world sounds that in some way express these links of feeling.

Ordinarily these things have been regarded rather superficially. It was thought that in speech we imitate the way an animal barks or growls. On this basis the famous linguistic bowwow theory was formulated, claiming that all speech is imitation. Such theories are dangerous in that they are quarter-truths. By copying a dog and saying 'bowwow' (which bears within it the feeling nuance expressed in the sound 'ow') I enter into the dog's condition of soul. The sound is formed not in accordance with the theory but in the more roundabout manner of placing myself in the dog's condition of soul. There is another theory which maintains that every object contains an inherent sound just as for instance a bell has its own sound. The so-called dingdong theory has arisen out of this assumption. The bowwow theory and the dingdong theory really do exist. But we cannot understand the human being unless we accept the fact that speech is the expression of the world of feeling, of the feeling links we form with the objects around us.

Another nuance of feeling we have towards objects is the one we have towards what is empty or what is black, for blackness is related to emptiness. This feeling nuance that we have towards everything related to blackness is the feeling of fear, of anxiety. This expresses itself in the 'U' (oo) sound. Towards what is full, on the other hand, and towards what is white and bright and all that is related to whiteness and brightness, and towards the sound that is related to brightness, we have the feeling nuance of wonder, admiration: the 'A' (father) sound. If we have the feeling that we must ward off an external impression, or in a way turn away from it to protect ourselves, if the feeling is one of offering resistance, this is expressed in the 'E' (eight) sound. And the opposite feeling of pointing towards, of approaching and becoming one with something is expressed in the 'I' (ee) sound.

These, then, are the main vowels. We shall go into all the details later, including the diphthongs. One other vowel should be considered; this is less frequent in European countries and expresses something stronger than all the others. If you try to find a vowel by letting 'A', 'O' and 'U' sound together, this expresses at first a feeling of fear but then an identification with what is feared. The profoundest awe is expressed by this sound. It is one that is especially frequent in Oriental languages and shows that Orientals are people able to develop a high degree of awe and veneration, while in Occidental languages this sound is missing because here we find people in whom awe and veneration are not their strongest point.

We now have a picture of the inner soul moods that come to expression in the vowels. All vowels express inner soul stirrings that live in the sympathy we have towards things. For even if we are afraid of something, this fear is founded on some mysterious sympathy. We would not be afraid of something if we did not have a hidden sympathy for it. In observing these things you must, however, take something into account: It is relatively easy to observe that the 'O' sound has something to do with astonishment, the 'U' sound with fear and anxiety, the 'A' sound with admiration and wonder, the 'E' sound with offering resistance, the 'I' sound with drawing near to something, and the 'AOU' sound with veneration. But your ability to observe is obscured because you easily confuse the feeling nuance you have when hearing the sound with the feeling nuance that arises when you speak the sound. The two are different. You must take into account that the nuances of feeling I have enumerated here are connected with the communication of the sounds. They apply if you want to communicate something to a person through the sound. If you want to tell someone that you have been afraid, this is expressed by the 'U' sound. There is a difference of nuance if you yourself are afraid or if you want to arouse fear in someone else by articulating the 'U' sound. You will receive an echo of your own fear if you want to arouse it in another, for instance by saying to a child: 'U-u-u'! (ooo). It is important to take this into account with regard to the social connotations of speech. If you do so you will easily arrive at this observation.

What is felt here is a pure inner soul process. This soul process, which is quite definitely based on the effect of sympathy, can be met from outside by antipathy. This occurs through the consonants. When we bring together a consonant and a vowel we mingle sympathy and antipathy, and our tongue, our lips and our palate are really present in order to make themselves felt as organs of antipathy, to ward things off. Were we to speak only in vowels, we should for ever be surrendering ourselves to things. We would actually merge into things and be extremely unegoistic, for we should unfold our deepest sympathy with everything; we would somewhat withdraw from things only in nuances of sympathy, for instance if we felt fear or horror, but even in this withdrawing from things there would be sympathy. Just as vowels are related to our own sounding, so consonants are related to things; the things sound with them.

Thus you will find that vowels have to be sought for as nuances of feeling, while consonants, F, B, M and so on, are sought as imitations of external things. So when I showed you the F related to the fish yesterday, what I did was right in that I imitated the external shape of the fish. It will always be possible to trace consonants to the imitation of external things while vowels on the contrary are quite elementary expressions of nuances of feeling in human beings towards things. Therefore you can quite well look upon speech as the confrontation between antipathy and sympathy. The sympathies always lie in the vowels and the antipathies always in the consonants.

We can also look upon the fashioning of speech in another way. We can ask: What kind of sympathy is it that comes to expression in the chest region of the human being in such a way that the chest region arrests antipathy and the head region only accompanies it? The foundation of this is in fact something musical that has passed beyond certain boundaries. Musicality is the foundation and it goes beyond certain limits; in a way it surpasses itself and becomes something more than musical. That is to say: Insofar as speech consists of vowels it encompasses something musical; and insofar as it consists of consonants it bears within itself something like sculpture or painting. In speech we have a genuine synthesis, a true uniting in the human being of the musical with the plastic element.

This shows us how with a kind of unconscious subtlety language reveals the nature not only of individuals but actually of human communities. In German the head is 'Kopf'. 'Kopf' expresses in every sense a roundness of form. 'Kopf' denotes not only the human head but also, for instance, a head of cabbage. Thus in the German word 'Kopf' the form is expressed. The Romance languages do not depict the form of the head. Here we find the word 'testa' which expresses something belonging to the soul realm. Here the fact is expressed that the head bears witness, testifies, identifies. The word for head thus comes from quite a different foundation. On the one hand a sympathetic feeling of the mind is expressed while on the other the fusion of antipathy with the external world is depicted. Let us try to determine the difference for the moment just with regard to the main vowels: 'Kopf', the 'O' sound = astonishment, amazement. The soul feels something of astonishment, amazement with regard to anything that is round because roundness itself is linked to everything that calls forth astonishment, amazement. Now look at 'testa', the 'E' sound = offering resistance. If someone else states something, we in turn have to assert ourselves and offer resistance or else we should simply merge and mingle with him. This nuance of feeling is very well expressed where it is the national characteristic to bring out the testifying, witnessing character of the head.

When you consider these things you are led away from the abstraction of looking to see what the dictionary says: this word for this language, that word for that language. The words in the different languages are in places taken from quite different connections. Merely to compare them is a purely external matter and to translate by the dictionary is on the whole the worst kind of translating. The German word 'Fuss' (foot) is connected with taking a step, making an empty space, a furrow ('Furche'). 'Fuss' is connected with 'Furche'. In German we take the foot and name it by what it does, namely making a furrow. The word for foot in the Romance languages, 'pes', is taken from standing firmly, having a standpoint. This study of languages, the linguistic study of meaning so extraordinarily helpful in teaching, does not yet exist on a scientific basis. We may well ask why these things are as yet not included in science even though they would be a real practical help.

The reason is that on the whole we are still in the process of working out what we need for the fifth post-Atlantean age, especially as regards education. If you take speech in this way to be indicating something inward in the vowels and something external in the consonants, you will find it quite easy to make pictures for the consonants. Then you will not need to use the pictures that I shall be giving you in the next few lectures; instead you will be able to make your own pictures and thus establish an inner contact with the children, which is much better than merely adopting the outer picture.

In this way we have recognized speech as a relationship between the human being and the cosmos. Man by himself would remain in astonishment, amazement; it is his relationship with the cosmos that calls forth sounds out of this astonishment, amazement.

Now man is embedded in the cosmos in a particular way and this can be observed by means of quite external considerations. What I now say is said because (as you will already have seen from yesterday's lecture) so much depends on the nature of our feelings towards the growing child, on how much we can really revere, in the growing human being, a mysterious revelation of the cosmos. A tremendous amount depends on our being able to develop this feeling as teachers and educators.

Adopting a broader view, let us now look once more at the significant fact that the human being takes approximately 18 breaths a minute. How many is this in 4 minutes? $18 \times 4 = 72$ breaths. How many breaths is it in a day? $18 \times 60 \times 24 = 25,920$ breaths in a day. I could also work this out in a different way by taking the number of breaths in 4 minutes, namely 72. Then instead of multiplying this by 24×60 I should only have to multiply it by 6×60, that is 360, and I should arrive at the same number of 25,920 breaths a day: $360 \times 72 = 25,920$. We can say: Our breathing process during the course of 4 minutes— breathing in, breathing out, breathing in, breathing out—is in a way a day in miniature. And the other sum of 25,920 obtained when we multiply it by 360 is in relation to this like the process of a whole year: the day of 24 hours is a year for our breathing.—Now let us turn to our greater breathing process which consists of the daily alternation between waking and sleeping. What, fundamentally, is waking and sleeping? Waking and sleeping also mean that we breathe something out and breathe something in. We breathe out our ego and our astral body when we go to sleep and we

breathe them in again when we wake up. We do this during
the course of 24 hours. In order to arrive at the sum of the
course of the year we have to multiply this day by 360. So
with this greater breathing process we complete in one year
something similar to what we achieve in one day with the
miniature breathing process, assuming that we multiply by
360 what takes place in 4 minutes. If we multiply by 360
what takes place with waking and sleeping during one day,
we have what takes place in one year; and if we now
multiply one year by our average life span, that is by 72, we
again arrive at 25,920. We have thus now discovered a
twofold breathing process: our in and out breathing that
takes place 72 times in 4 minutes and 25,920 times in one
day, and our waking and sleeping that takes place 360 times
in one year and 25,920 times during the course of a lifetime.
In addition to these there is a third breathing process to be
found if we follow the course of the sun. You know that the
spot where the sun rises in spring apparently advances
slightly each year. During the course of 25,920 years the sun
moves gradually round the whole ecliptic. So here once
again we have the number 25,920 in the planetary cosmic
year.

How is our life embedded in the universe? We live on the
average for 72 years. If you multiply this by 360 you arrive
once again at the figure of 25,920. You can thus imagine
that in the Platonic year, the cosmic revolution of the sun
that takes 25,920 years to come full circle, our human
lifespan is as one day. So we in our human life can regard as
one breath what in the universe is depicted as a year, while
seeing our human lifespan as a day in the great cosmic year;
thus we can revere the smallest process as an image of the
great cosmic process. Looking at the whole process more
closely, we find in the Platonic year, that is in what happens
during the course of the Platonic year, an image of the
whole process taking place from the old Saturn evolution

through the Sun, Moon and Earth evolutions and so on right up to the Vulcan evolution. All the processes that take place in the way indicated are ordered as breathing processes connected with the figure 25,920. And in what takes place for us between waking up and going to sleep we find once again an expression of all that occurred during the ancient Moon evolution, what is now occurring during the Earth evolution and what will occur during the Jupiter evolution. An expression is here found of all that makes us members of what is beyond the earth. And that which works to make us earthly men takes place in our smallest breathing process; we are human beings belonging to ancient Moon, to Earth and to Jupiter in our alternation between waking and sleeping; and through our lifespan we are cosmic human beings embedded in the conditions of the universal year. For cosmic life, for the whole planetary system, one day of our lives is just one breath. And all the 72 years of our life are just one day for the being whose organs are the planetary system. Overcome the illusion that you are a limited human being; conceive of yourself as a process in the cosmos, which is the reality, and you will be able to say: I am myself a breath drawn by the universe.

If you comprehend this in such a way that the theoretical aspect remains a matter of complete indifference to you, being merely a process that quite interested you in passing; if, though, you take away with you a feeling, a sense of immeasurable reverence for what expresses itself so mysteriously in every human being, then this sense will become in you the solid foundation that must underlie teaching and education. In the education of the future we cannot proceed by merely bringing external adult life into our teaching. It is truly fearful to contemplate the possibility that in future democratically elected parliaments will meet and proceed to make decisions on questions of teaching and education based on the recommendations of those whose sole claim to involvement in the matter is their democratic sense. If things were to develop in the way they are doing in Russia at the moment, this would mean that the Earth would lose its task, would have its mission withdrawn, would be expelled from the universe and fall prey to Ahriman.

The time has now come for man to derive what belongs to education from his knowledge of the relationship between man and the cosmos. We must permeate all our teaching with the feeling: the growing human being stands before us, but he is a continuation of what took place in the supersensible world before he was born or conceived. This feeling must grow out of the kind of recognition we arrived at just now after our consideration of the vowels and consonants. This feeling must permeate us completely. Only if we really are permeated by this feeling will we be able to teach properly. For do not imagine that this feeling could be fruitless! The human being is organized in such a way that if his feelings are properly oriented he derives from them his own guiding powers. If you are unable to win through to seeing every human being as a cosmic riddle, you will merely achieve the feeling that every person is a mechanism. And the cultivation of this feeling that man is only a mechanism would lead to the downfall of earthly culture. The rise of earthly culture, however, can only be sought in permeating our educational impulse with a feeling for the cosmic significance of the whole human being. But this cosmic feeling only arises for us if we regard what lies in human feeling as belonging to the period between birth and death. What lies in human thinking indicates the period before birth, and what lies in human willing points towards what will come after death, the germ of the future. With the threefold human being before us we see first of all what belongs to the time before birth, then what lies between birth and death, and thirdly what awaits after death; the pre-natal life enters our existence in images, whereas the germ of what belongs to the time after death is already in us before death.

It is only through such facts as these that you can gain some idea of what really happens when one human being forms a relationship with another. Reading older works on education, for instance the pedagogics of *Herbart*,[4] which was excellent in its day, we invariably feel: These people are working with concepts through which they cannot possibly reach the world; they remain outside reality. Consider only how sympathy, properly developed in the earthly sense, permeates all willing, in other words how the germ of the future, belonging to the time after death and lying in us as a consequence of the will, is permeated by love, by sympathy. Therefore also in education everything will in a way—or rather not in a way but quite definitely—have to be watched especially lovingly so that it can be checked or cultivated in the right way. We shall have to assist the sympathy already in the child by appealing to his will. What, then, will the real impulse for the education of the will have to be? It can be nothing other than the sympathy we have to develop for our pupil. The better the sympathy we develop with him, the better will be our educational methods.

Now you will say: Since educating the thinking is the opposite of educating the will because it is permeated with antipathy, must we now develop antipathies when we educate the thinking, the intellect of our pupil? Indeed you must, but you must understand this in the right way. You must place the antipathies on the proper footing. You must endeavour properly to understand the pupil himself if you want to educate him rightly for the life of thinking. This comprehending contains within itself the element of antipathy, for it belongs at this end of the scale. By comprehending your pupil, by endeavouring to penetrate all the nuances of his being, you become the educator, the teacher

of his understanding, his faculty of knowledge. The antipathies lie in this very activity; but you make the antipathy
good because you educate your pupil. Furthermore you can
be quite certain that we are not led to meet in this life if
there are no preconditions for it. Such external processes are
always actually the external expression of something inward, however strange this may seem to an external view of
the world. The fact that you are here to teach and educate
these children from the Waldorf factory and do whatever is
necessary in this connection indicates that this group of
teachers and this group of children belong together karmic-
ally. And you become the right teacher for these children
through having in former times developed antipathies
towards these children; now you free yourself from these
antipathies by educating the thinking of these children. And
we must develop sympathies in the right way by bringing
about the right development of the will.

So be quite clear about this: You will best be able to
penetrate into the twofold being of man in the manner
attempted in our seminar discussion.[5] But you must
endeavour to penetrate into all aspects of the human being.
Through what we attempted in the seminar[6] you will
become a good educator only of the thought life of the child.
For his will life you will be a good educator if you
endeavour to surround every individual with sympathy,
with real sympathy. These things also belong to education:
Antipathy that enables us to comprehend and sympathy
that enables us to love. In that we have a body in which
there are centres where sympathy and antipathy meet, this
also enters that aspect of social intercourse between people
which expresses itself in educating and teaching. I beg you
to think this through and take it into your feelings; then we
shall be able to continue tomorrow.

LECTURE THREE

Stuttgart, 23 August 1919

I pointed out yesterday[7] that our teaching should proceed in the first place from a certain artistic formative quality so that the whole being of the child, particularly his will life, can be called into play in the lessons. From the discussions we have had here you will have no difficulty in understanding the importance of such measures and you will also grasp that unceasing account must be taken of the fact that in the human being there is something dead, something dying that must be transmuted into something newly living. If we approach the beings of nature and the world at large merely as onlookers with our understanding that works in mental pictures, we stand rather within a dying process; if we approach these beings of nature and the world with our will, we stand in an enlivening process. As educators we shall thus have the task of constantly quickening what is dead and protecting what is approaching death in the human being from dying entirely; indeed, we shall have to fructify this dying with the quickening element we develop out of the will. Therefore we must not be apprehensive about starting right from the beginning with a certain artistic form in our lessons while the children are still young.

Now everything artistic that comes towards mankind is divided into two streams, the sculptural, pictorial stream and the musical, poetic stream. These two streams of art, the sculptural and pictorial and the musical and poetic, are indeed polar opposites, though just because of their polarity they are also especially capable of a higher synthesis, a higher union. You obviously know that this duality in the artistic realm even finds expression racially in world evolution. You need only remind yourselves of certain writings of *Heinrich Heine*[8] and your attention will be drawn to this duality: All that emanates from the Greek peoples or is related to them, all that has grown from the being of the Greek peoples in a manner suited to their race is in the most exalted sense a disposition directed towards the sculptural, pictorial formation of the world; and all that emanates from the Jewish element is disposed towards the musical element of the world. Thus we find these two streams divided even racially and those who are receptive to such things will have no difficulty in tracing this in the history of art. Naturally and quite justifiably there are always efforts to unite the musical with the sculptural and pictorial. However, they may only be entirely united in eurythmy when it is fully developed so that the musical and the visible can become one. I do not of course mean the beginnings of eurythmy we are working with now but the ultimate aims there must be in eurythmy. We must, then, take into account that there is in the totality of harmonious human nature a sculptural, pictorial element towards which man's will tends to be oriented. How can we properly characterize this tendency in man to become sculptural and pictorial?

If we were solely beings of understanding, were we to observe the world only through our mental pictures, we should gradually become walking corpses. Here on earth we would indeed give the impression of dying beings. We save ourselves from this mortality only by feeling in ourselves the urge to quicken with our sculptural and pictorial imagination what is dying in concepts. If you wish to be true educators you must be on your guard against making everything abstractly uniform. Thus you must not allow yourselves to say: We should not develop the death processes in man; we must avoid training the conceptual world of ideas in the children.—This would be the same mistake in the realm of the soul and spirit as if doctors were to observe cultural evolution as though they were great pedagogues and then pronounce: The bones are the dying part of the human being; let us therefore guard him against this dying element; let us endeavour to keep the bones living and soft.—The opinion of such physicians would lead to a population of rickety human beings unable to fulfil their tasks properly. It is always wrong to proceed after the manner of many theosophists and anthroposophists who speak of Ahriman and Lucifer and their influence on mankind's development saying: These are things that damage the nature of man; therefore we must guard against them.—This would lead to the exclusion of man from everything that ought to constitute him. So we cannot prevent the education of the conceptual, thinking element; we must educate it, but we must also never fail at other times to approach the nature of the child through the sculptural and pictorial element. Out of this, unity arises. It does not arise by means of extinguishing one element but out of the development of both side by side. In this respect people today cannot yet think in terms of unity. That is why they cannot understand the threefold ordering of the social organism.[9] For social life it is entirely right that the spiritual, the economic and the rights spheres should stand side by side and that unity then comes about, instead of being constructed abstractly. Imagine what it would mean if people were to say: Because the head is a unit and the rest of the body also, the human being ought not really to exist; we should form the head away from the rest of the human being and let it move about the world freely! We follow the creativity of nature only when we allow the whole to arise out of all the onesided parts.

So it is a matter of developing the one side: mental, conceptual education; then the other side, the sculptural,

pictorial element, quickens what is unfolded in the merely
conceptual. We are concerned, in this age that always seeks
to destroy consciousness, with raising these things into our
awareness without losing our naivety. We need not lose it if
we build things up in a concrete and not an abstract way. It
would in every way be very good if we could, for instance,
start as early as possible with regard to the sculptural,
pictorial element, letting the child live in the world of
colour, and also if we as teachers would steep ourselves in
what *Goethe* presents in the didactic part of his *Theory of
Colours*.[10] It is founded on the way Goethe always permeates
each individual colour with a nuance of feeling. Thus he
emphasizes the challenging nature of red; he stresses not
only what the eye sees but also what the soul feels in the
red. Similarly he emphasizes the stillness and absorption the
soul feels in blue. It is possible, without piercing the child's
naivety, to lead him into the world of colour in a way that
lets the feeling nuances of this world of colour emerge in a
living way. If to start with the result is a great deal of mess,
it will be a good educational measure to train the child to be
less messy.

We should introduce the child to colours as early as
possible and it is good to let him use coloured paints on
coloured as well as white surfaces. And we should endeavour
to awaken in the child the kind of feelings that can arise
only out of a spiritual scientific view of the world of colour.[11]
Working in the way I have done with friends in the small
dome of the Dornach building,[12] one gains a living relationship to colour. One discovers, for instance, when using blue,
that it lies within the blue colour itself to characterize the
whole realm of inward absorption. So if we want to paint an
angel moved by inwardness, we quite automatically have
the urge to use blue because the nuances of blue, the light
and dark of blue call forth in the soul a feeling of movement
arising out of the soul element. A yellow-reddish colour calls

up in the soul the sensation of shining, of outward revelation. So if the effect of something is aggressive, if there is an exhortation, if the angel desires to speak to us, if he wants to emerge from his background and speak, then we express this in the yellow-reddish nuances. It is perfectly possible in an elementary way to show children this inherent livingness of colours.

Next we must come to be very sure in ourselves that plain drawing has something untrue about it. The truest of all is the feeling that comes from the colour itself, somewhat untrue is the feeling that comes from light and dark, and the least true of all is drawing. Drawing as such does indeed approach the abstract element that is present in nature as something dying. We should really draw only in a way that makes us aware that we are drawing essentially what is dead. And painting with colours we should do in a way that

makes us aware: we are calling forth the living out of the dead. What is, after all, the line of an horizon? If we simply take a pencil and draw an horizon line, it is something abstract, death dealing, untrue over against nature which always has two streams, the dead and the living. We are merely paring off one of the streams and saying that that is nature. If, on the other hand, I say that I can see something green and something blue that are adjacent but separate, then the line of the horizon grows where the two colours meet and I am saying something that is true. In this way you will gradually come to appreciate that the forms of nature really arise out of the colours and that therefore drawing is a process of abstraction. We should create in the growing child a good mental picture and feeling for such things because this quickens his whole soul being, creating

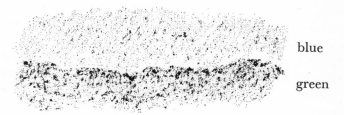

blue

green

for it a right relationship with the external world. The reason for the sickness of our culture is that we have no proper relationship with the external world. In teaching in this way there is no need for us to become onesided. It would, for instance, be rather good if we could gradually develop the possibility of passing from purely abstract artistic work, such as the human being creates out of his delight in beauty, to concrete art, artistic craftsmanship. Mankind today is urgently in need of really artistic crafts that can find their place in general cultural life. During the course of the nineteenth century we actually finally reached the point at which we made our furniture to please the eye; we made a chair, for instance, that could delight the eye, whereas in fact a chair should have an inherent character that we feel when we sit upon it. This is what ought to govern the shaping of the chair. A chair should not be merely beautiful; it should invite us to feel our way into it; it should have an inherent character that makes it suitable for a person to sit upon. By the manner in which the arms are attached to the chair, and so on, when a person seeks support from it, the chair should express its growing together with our sense of touch, even our cultivated sense of touch. We should be doing today's culture a great service if we were to introduce artistic craft lessons into the educational system. Consider how those of us who desire the best for mankind are seized today by a tremendous anxiety concerning our culture when we see, for instance, how abstractions (this will not happen if we succeed in achieving our aims), how the primitive ideas of people with socialistic tendencies are threatening to flood our culture. Nothing will be beautiful in our civilization any more, only utilitarian! And even if people dream of beauty, they will have no feeling for the urgency with which we shall have to stress the necessity for the beautiful the more we drift towards socialism. This must be recognized.

So we should not be sparing with the sculptural, pictorial element in our lessons. In the same way we should not be sparing in our efforts to create a genuine feeling for that dynamic element that finds expression in architecture. It will be very easy to make the mistake of approaching the children with one aspect or another too early. But in some ways it is in fact right if this happens. It fell to me to say a few words to the eighty children from Munich who have been spending their holidays in Dornach where Frau Kisseleff[13] gave them twelve eurythmy lessons; they demonstrated to some of their teachers and the Dornach anthroposophists what they had learnt. The children were very keen and after the end of the performance, which included some items by our Dornach eurythmists, they crowded round asking: Did you like our performance? They really wanted to perform well; the whole incident was most heartwarming. Now the people who had arranged the whole event had asked me to say a few words to the children. It was the evening before their return to Munich. I said literally: Now I am going to say something that you will not yet understand. You will understand it later on. Pay attention in the future when you hear the word 'soul', for now you cannot understand it yet.—It is extraordinarily important to draw attention in this way to things the child cannot yet understand. The principle so much in force today, that one should teach the child only what it understands, is wrong. It is a principle that makes all education lifeless. Education comes to life only if what is taken in is carried for a while in the depths and then brought back to the surface later. This is most important for education between the seventh and fifteenth years; a great deal can be allowed to trickle into the child's soul which cannot be understood till later. Please do not feel it is wrong to overstep the child's maturity by touching on things he will only be able to understand later. The contrary principle has brought something deadening into our system of teaching. The child, however, must know that he will have to wait. It is possible to awaken in him this feeling that he must wait until he can understand something he is absorbing. In this sense it was not all bad when in the past children were made to learn by rote $1 \times 1 = 1$, $2 \times 2 = 4$, $3 \times 3 = 9$ and so on instead of learning as they do today with the help of an abacus. We ought to break through this principle of holding back the child's understanding. This can of course only be done with the necessary tact for we must not be at too great a remove from what the child can love; yet he can become permeated, simply on the authority of his teacher, with a great deal that he will not be able to understand till later.

If you bring the sculptural, pictorial element towards the child in this way, you will find yourself able to quicken much of what is deadening.

The musical element that lives in man from birth and that, as I have already said, finds particular expression during the third and fourth years as an inclination to dance, is inherently a will element carrying life within it. Yet strange though this may sound, in the way it expresses itself in the child to start with it carries life too strongly, life that is too stunning and easily benumbs consciousness. This strong musical element very easily brings about a certain dazed state in the child's development. Therefore we have to say: The educational influence we exert by using the musical element must consist in a constant harmonizing by the Apollonian element of the Dionysian element welling up out of man's nature. While it is a deadening influence that has to be quickened by the sculptural, pictorial element, something that is alive in the highest degree in the musical element has to be damped down so that in music it does not affect the human being too strongly.—This is the feeling with which we ought to bring music to the children.

Now the fact is that human nature is developed by karma with a bias towards one side or another. This is particularly noticeable in connection with the musical element. But I should like to point out that it is too much emphasized. We should not stress so sharply: This is an unmusical child, and this one is musical.—The differences do in fact exist, but to take them to their ultimate consequence of excluding the unmusical child from everything musical and giving musical education only to children with musical inclinations, is most definitely wrong. At the very least even the most unmusical children must be present whenever anything musical is done. It is right, of course, that as far as musical perform-ances are concerned there will be an increasing involve-ment only of those children who are really musical. But the unmusical children should always be there and their recep-tivity to music should be developed; for you will notice that even the most unmusical child possesses a remnant of musical talent which is merely rather deeply buried and can only be raised by a loving approach. This should never be neglected, for it is far truer than we imagine that, in Shakespeare's words[14]: The man that hath no music in himself . . . is fit for treasons, stratagems and spoils; . . . let no such man be trusted!—This is a very fundamental truth. Therefore no effort should be spared in bringing the musical element even to those children who are considered at first to be unmusical.

Of greatest importance, just in relation to our social life, will be the fostering of music in an elementary way through

teaching the children straight out of the musical facts without any bemusing theory. The children should gain a clear
idea of elementary music, of harmonies, melodies and so on
through the application of elementary facts, through the
analysing by ear of melodies and harmonies, so that with
music we build up the whole artistic realm in the same
elementary way as we do the sculptural, pictorial realm
where we similarly work up from the details. This will help
to mitigate the amateurishness that plays such a part in
music; mind you, it cannot be denied that musical dilettantism does serve a certain purpose in the social life of the
community. Without it we should not progress particularly
well. But it should be confined to the listeners. If this could
be achieved, it would be possible for those who perform and
produce music to find their proper recognition within our
social order. For we should not forget that everything in the
sculptural, pictorial realm works towards the individualizing
of the human being, while all that is musical and poetical
fosters our social life. Human beings are brought together as
one through music and poetry; they become individuals
through sculpture and painting. The individuality is sup-
ported more by the sculptural, pictorial element, and society
more by the living and weaving in community through
music and poetry. Poetry is conceived out of the solitude of
the soul—there alone; and it is comprehended through the
community of mankind. It is entirely concrete, not at all
abstract, to assert that with the poetry a man creates he
reveals his inner being and that this is met by the deepest
inner being of another human being when the latter takes in
the created work. Therefore delight in music and poetry and
also yearning for them should be encouraged in the growing
child. As regards poetry, the child should early on come to
know what is truly poetical. Today we grow up into a social
order in which we are tyrannized by the prose element of
speech. Countless reciters today tyrannize people with prose

by giving first place to the prose element in poetry, in other words merely to the actual meaning. When a poem is presented in a manner that gives pride of place to the nuances of content, this is regarded nowadays as faultless recitation. Really perfect recitation, however, stresses the musical element. In the introductions I sometimes give to eurythmy performances,[15] I have several times pointed out how with a poet like *Schiller*[16] a poem emerges from the depths of his soul. With many of his poems an undefined melody first held sway in his soul and he only later as it were immersed the content, the actual words, into this undefined melody. The content is suspended in the general melody and the creative poetic activity is then the forming of the language, not the content, the forming of the beat, the rhythm, the rhyme, in other words the musical element on which poetry is founded. I said that people are tyrannized by the modern manner of recitation because it is always an act of tyranny to place the main emphasis on the prose, the content of a poem taken quite abstractly. In spiritual science we can only supersede this tyranny by depicting, as I always endeavour to do, a subject from the most varied viewpoints so that, also artistically, our concepts remain fluid. It gave me particular pleasure to be told one day by one of our artistically gifted friends that some of the lecture cycles I have given could be transcribed into symphonies purely on the basis of their inner structure. Some of the courses are indeed based in their structure on something very like this. Take for instance the course given in Vienna on life between death and a new birth[17]: you will see that you could make a symphony of it. This is possible because a lecture concerning spiritual science should not work tyrannically but should arouse people's will. Yet when they meet something like *The Threefold Social Order* they say it is incomprehensible. It is not incomprehensible; it is only the manner of its presentation to which they are unaccustomed.

It is therefore exceedingly important to draw the child's attention to the musical element on which every poem is founded. So the lessons should be arranged in a way that allows the element of recitation in the school to come as close as possible to the musical element. The music teacher should be in close contact with the teacher who gives recitation so that one may follow directly on the other and so that a living relationship between the two is established. It would be particularly useful if the music teacher could stay on when the recitation teacher takes over and vice versa, so that the one could continue to point out the links with the other. This would be a means of thoroughly eliminating something really dreadful that is still very much prevalent in our schools: the abstract explanation of poems. This abstract explanation of poetry, verging almost on grammatical dissection, spells the death of everything that ought to work on the child. The interpreting of poems is something quite appalling.

Now you will protest that interpretation is necessary if the children are to understand the poem. The answer to that is: All the lessons must be structured to form a totality. This has to be discussed in the weekly meetings of the teachers. If this or that poem is to be recited, then the other lessons must include whatever might be necessary for its understanding. Care must be taken that the children bring to the recitation lesson whatever they need to help them understand the poem. If, for instance, Schiller's *Spaziergang* is to be recited, the cultural and historical and also the psychological aspects of the poem can quite easily be presented to the children, not by going through the poem line by line but simply by telling them whatever they need to know about the content. In the recitation lesson itself the only important thing is the artistic presentation of something artistic.

If we were to use art in its two streams in this way to

harmonize human nature through and through, we should indeed achieve a tremendous amount. Consider alone the fact that something infinitely important in man's harmony with the world is achieved when he sings. Singing is a way of reproducing what is already present in the world. When the human being sings he expresses the momentous wisdom out of which the world is built. We must also not forget that in singing man links the cosmic element of the actual sequence of notes with the human word. This brings something unnatural into singing. We can feel this even in the incompatibility of the sound of a poem with its content. It would be a step in the right direction if we could develop further the endeavours we have just started, namely to present each line in recitative form and quicken only the rhyming word with melody, so that the line flows along in recitative[18] and the rhyming word is sung like an aria. This would ensure a clear distinction between the sounding of a poem and the words which actually disturb the musical part of man.

And again, when the musical ear of the individual is cultivated he is induced to experience in a living way the musical essence of the world itself. This is of the utmost value for the developing human being. We must not forget: In the sculptural, pictorial realm we look at beauty, we live it, whereas in the musical realm we ourselves become beauty. This is extraordinarily significant. The further you go back to ancient times, the less you find there what we call musical. We can have the distinct impression that music is something still in the process of becoming, even though some musical forms are already dying out again. This is founded on a most significant cosmic fact. In all sculptural and pictorial art man has been the imitator of the old celestial order. The highest imitation of a cosmic celestial order is an imitation of the world in sculpture or painting. But in music man himself is the creator. He creates some-

thing that does not come from what is already there but lays
the foundation and firm ground for what is to arise in the
future. Of course a certain musicality can be created by
simply imitating in music the sighing of the waves or the
singing of the nightingale. But all real music and real poetry
is a new creation and it is out of this creating anew that the
Jupiter, Venus and Vulcan evolutions of the world will arise
later. By starting with music we in some way rescue what
still has to come about; we rescue it for reality out of the
present nullity of its existence.

Not until we link ourselves in this way to the great facts of
the universe do we gain a real understanding of what
teaching means. Only out of such an understanding can the
right solemnity emerge so that teaching really becomes a
kind of service to God, a consecrated service.

What I thus present to you will be more or less an ideal.
But surely what we do in practice can be included in the
ideal. There is something, for instance, that we must not
neglect when we take the children we teach (which we shall
certainly do) out into the mountains or the fields, in other
words when we take them out into nature. Over against this
taking of the children out into nature we must always
remember that lessons on natural science have their right
place only inside the classroom. Let us assume that we step
with the children out into nature where we draw their
attention to a stone or a flower. In doing so we should
strictly avoid any allusion to what we teach inside the
classroom. Out of doors in natural surroundings we should
draw the children's attention to nature in a way that is
totally different from the method we use in the classroom.
We should never forget to point out to them: We take you
out into the open so that you may feel the beauty of nature
and we bring the products of nature into the classroom so
that indoors we can dissect and analyse nature.—Thus we
should never speak to the children out of doors on what we

show them indoors, for instance about the plants. We should emphasize how different it is to dissect dead nature in the classroom or to look upon the beauty of nature out of doors. We should compare these two experiences. It is not right to take the children outside into nature in order to use natural objects to exemplify what we have taught them in the classroom. The kind of feeling we should seek to arouse in the children is: Unfortunately we have to dissect nature when we bring it into the classroom.—But the children should nevertheless feel this as a necessity, for the destruction of what is natural is also necessary in the building up of the human being. We should certainly not imagine that we are doing any good by giving a scientific explanation of a beetle out of doors in natural surroundings. The scientific description of the beetle belongs in the classroom! When we take the children out into the open we have to arouse in them delight at the sight of the beetle, delight in the way he runs about, in his drollness, delight in his relationship to the rest of nature. Furthermore we should not neglect to call forth in the child's soul a clear sense of how something creative lies in music, something transcending nature, and of how man himself shares in the creation of nature when he develops music. This will be formed as a feeling only very primitively of course, but it will be the first that must emerge from the will element of music: that the human being feels himself within the cosmos!

LECTURE FOUR

Stuttgart, 25 August 1919

Building on the kind of feeling that may arise from the considerations we discussed just now in our session on general education,[19] I should like to start with a point of method that is exceedingly important and that moreover links up with the discussions on aspects of method we have had so far.

You must look on the first lesson you have with your pupils in every class as outstandingly important. In a certain sense something far more important will emanate from this first lesson than from all the others. Of course these other lessons will then have to be turned to account so that what emanates from the first lesson can become fruitful for all the others. Let us now imagine quite practically how we shall shape this very first lesson, for soon you will be making the acquaintance of the children who will bring with them the consequences of every kind of upbringing both good and bad. Naturally I can only make general suggestions here which you will be able to develop further. The point is that you will not have to follow the misguided educational principles that have come to the fore lately; what you must do is concern yourselves with whatever has genuine significance for the child's development.

You are faced, then, with your class of all sorts of children. The first thing to do is to draw their attention to the reason why they are there in the classroom. It is ever so important that you should speak to the children somewhat in this vein: So you have come to school, and now I am

55

going to tell you why you have come to school.—This act of coming to school should immediately be brought to their consciousness: You have come to school in order to learn something. You have as yet no idea of all the things you will be learning in school, but there will be all sorts of things that you will have to learn. Why will you have to learn all sorts of different things in school? Well, you have no doubt met some adults, some grown-up people, and you must have noticed that they can do something that you cannot do. And so that one day you will also be able to do what the grown-ups can do is the reason why you are here. One day you will be able to do something that you cannot do yet.—It is most important to work through this network of thoughts with the children. And these thoughts lead on to yet something else.

No teaching can flow in the right channels unless it is accompanied by a certain respect for the previous generation. However much this nuance must remain in the realm of feeling and sensing, we must nevertheless cultivate in the children by every means a respect and reverence with which they look up to what former generations have already achieved and what they are also meant to achieve by going to school. We must from the start arouse in the children this way of regarding the culture of their environment with a certain respect so that they do actually see those people who are older as somewhat higher beings. If this feeling is not aroused there is no progress in teaching and education. Similarly no progress is made if we do not raise into the consciousness of the children's souls what is expected to happen. Proceed to reflect with the children, then, without hesitation that in so doing you are looking beyond their horizon. It does not matter, you see, if you say a great deal to the child that he will only understand later. The principle that you should only teach the child what he can understand and form an opinion on is the principle that has

ruined so much in our culture. The very well known teacher
of an even better known contemporary personality once
boasted of having educated his pupil according to the
following principle: He said that he had trained the boy
well, for he had forced him always to form an immediate
opinion on everything. Well, very many people today agree
with this principle of forming an immediate opinion and it is
not remarkable that a very well known teacher of an even
better known personality should stress the wish to emphasize
it in books on education. In connection with this principle I
have actually come across the statement in a modern work
on education that we can but hope for the possibility of
providing such exemplary education for every German boy
and girl. You will gather from this that you can find in
modern works on education a great deal of what ought not
to be done, for there is a great tragedy in this kind of
education, and this tragedy in its turn is linked with the
present world catastrophe.

The point is therefore not that the child should immediately form opinions on everything but that between his
seventh and fifteenth years he should learn what he has to
learn out of love for his teacher, out of a sense of his
teacher's authority. Therefore the suggested conversation
with the children, which you can expand on as you wish,
should continue something like this: Look how grown-ups
have books and can read. You can't read yet, but you will
learn to read and when you have learnt how to do it you
will also be able to take the books and learn from them what
the grown-ups can learn from them. Grown-ups can write
letters to each other, in fact they can write down anything
they like. Later on you will also be able to write letters, for
as well as learning to read you will also learn to write. As
well as reading and writing, grown-ups can also do sums.
You don't yet know what doing sums means. But you have
to be able to do sums when you go out into life, for instance

if you want to buy something to eat or to wear, or if you want to make something to wear.—This is the kind of conversation you must have with the children. Then you say: You will also learn to do sums.—It is a good thing to draw the children's attention to this, and then perhaps straight away the next day to draw their attention to it again, so that you repeat the whole matter a number of times. It is important, then, to raise into consciousness what the children do in this way.

Altogether it is most important in teaching and education to bring—if I may put it this way—consciously into consciousness what otherwise goes on in life through force of habit. In contrast, no advantage is gained for teaching and education by including in the lesson all sorts of things merely for the purpose of the lesson, or even only seemingly for the purpose of the lesson. You may meet the recommendation that children should come to school armed with a box full of spent matches so that they may be taught how to make patterns with them—of course the matches should if possible be square and not round so that they do not roll off the sloping desks! The children are taught, for instance, how to lay the matches in the shape of a house and so on. Match laying is quite a favourite subject highly recommended for little children. In contrast with a real knowledge of life such things are nothing but a way of playing about; learning something by laying match-sticks in patterns has no meaning for the being of man. Whatever the laying of match-sticks in patterns might lead to can only be regarded by people in later life as playing about. It is not good to introduce mere playing about into education. On the contrary, it is our task to introduce the fullness of life into education; we should not bring in things that are no more than playing about. But please do not misunderstand me. I am not saying that play should not be introduced into education; what I mean is that games artificially constructed for the lesson have no place in school. There will still be a great deal to say about how play can be incorporated into the lessons.

How, then, can we really work effectively, particularly in the forming of the will right from the start?

After discussing sufficiently with the children what I have been demonstrating, namely on the one hand what is intended to help them develop an awareness of why they have come to school and on the other hand what is meant to help them attain a certain respect and admiration for adults, the time will have come to move on to something else. It is then good, for instance, to say: Look at yourselves. You have two hands, a left one and a right one. These hands are for working, you can do all kinds of things with them.—In this way you also raise into consciousness what belongs to the human being. The child should not just know that he has hands but he should be conscious of the fact that he has hands. Naturally you may be tempted to say that the child is of course aware of having hands. But it is different if he knows that he has hands with which to work or if this thought has never crossed his mind. Having spoken with the children for a while about their hands and about working with their hands, we then proceed to letting them do something skilful with their hands. This might even take place in the very first lesson. You might say to them: Watch me do this (see left-hand drawing). Now take your hand and do it too! Now we let the children do the same, as slowly as possible. Actually it will be a slow process if we call the children up one by one to the blackboard, letting them make their mark on the board and then return to their seats. The most important thing is that they should digest the lesson properly. Then you might say to the children: Now I am going to do this (see right-hand drawing). And now you can take your hands and do it too.—Each child then does this too. When they have all finished you say: This one is a

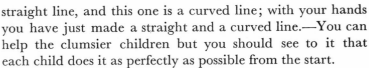

straight line, and this one is a curved line; with your hands
you have just made a straight and a curved line.—You can
help the clumsier children but you should see to it that
each child does it as perfectly as possible from the start.

So right from the start we let the children do something,
and we must make sure that in subsequent lessons this is
repeated a number of times. Thus in the following lesson we
let the children make a straight line and then a curved line.
Now let us consider a subtle distinction. You need at first
attach no great value to letting the children make a straight
and a curved line from memory; once again you first make
the straight line on the board and let the children copy it,
and the same with the curved line. Then you ask individual
children: What is that?—A straight line! What is that?—A
curved line! You thus use the principle of repetition by
letting the children copy the drawing and then, without
repeating it yourself first, letting them name it themselves. It
is most important to use this subtle nuance. Altogether you
must make great efforts to cultivate the habit of doing the
right things in front of the children; the educational maxims
you believe in must become second nature to you.

You need not hesitate at all quite early on to take out a
box of paints and set a glass of water beside it (indeed it is a
particularly good idea to do such things quite soon with the
children). After you have pinned a white surface to the
blackboard with drawing pins you take up a brush, dip it in
the water, take some paint and make a small yellow patch

on the white surface. When you have done this you let each child come to the blackboard and make a similar small patch. Each patch must be separate from the others so that in the end you have so and so many yellow patches. Then you dip your brush in the blue paint and put some blue next to your yellow patch. And you let the children come and put on some blue in the same way. When about half of them have done so you say: Now we shall do something else; I am going to dip my brush in the green paint and put green next to the other yellow patches.—Avoiding as well as you can making them jealous of each other, you then let the remaining children put on the green in the same way. All this will take a while. The children will digest it well. It is indeed essential to proceed very slowly, taking only very few small steps in the lesson. Now the time has come for you to say: I am going to tell you something that you will not yet understand very well, but one day you will understand it quite well: what we did at the top, where we put blue next to the yellow, is more beautiful than what we did at the bottom, where we put green next to the yellow!—This will sink deeply into the child's soul. It will be necessary to return to it with him several times in repetition, but he will also puzzle away at it himself; he will not be entirely indifferent to it but will learn to understand quite well from simple, naive examples how to feel the difference between something beautiful and something less beautiful.

A similar method can be used when you introduce music into the lesson. It is good here too to start from one note or another. There is no need to tell the children the name of the note. You simply strike the note in some way. It is good then to let the children also strike the note, thus here too combining the lesson with the will element. Afterwards you strike a second, concordant note and then let a number of the children strike it too. The next step is to strike a note followed by a discordant note and again let the children do the same. You try, just as before with the colours, to awaken in the children a feeling for the concordance and discordance of notes not by talking to them about concordance and discordance but by speaking of beautiful and less beautiful, thus appealing here also to their feelings. These things, and not the letters of the alphabet, are the starting points for the early lessons. With these things we should start.

Now let us turn our attention first to the class teacher. He will hold with the children the conversations I have just described. Perhaps the musical element will have to be treated separately and introduced to the children in another lesson. It will then be good if the music teacher could conduct a very similar conversation, though oriented more towards the musical and if he too could go over the same ground more than once. From this the children will discover that the same things are repeated not only by one teacher but also by another so that they find they are learning the same from both teachers. This should help to give the school a more corporative character. In their weekly meetings the teachers should discuss all these things so as to bring about a certain unity in the lessons.

Only when you have taught the children in this way to use their hands and ears is the time ripe for progressing to the first elements of reading, in fact particularly the reading of handwriting. (We shall pay greater attention to the details later. Today in this preparatory talk, rather than pedantically examining one aspect after another I want to bring up the points of view according to which we can proceed.) As regards method, it will have had an extraordinarily good effect on the children to have spoken to them as early as the first lesson about writing, reading and arithmetic and how they cannot do these things yet but will learn them all in school. As a result of this the hope, the wish, the resolve form in the child and through what you yourself do he finds his way into a world of feeling that in turn acts as an incentive to the realm of the will. So this too you can do: as an educational measure you do not present the children directly with what you want to teach them; instead you leave them for a while in a state of expectation. This has an extraordinarily good effect on the development of the will in the growing human being.

Before going into this in more detail I now want to dispel certain ideas you may have that could cause confusion. So many sins have been committed through the prevailing methods of learning reading and writing, but especially in what is, after all, connected with learning to read and write: language teaching, grammar, syntax and so on. There has been so much sinning that there are doubtless few people who do not remember with some horror the lessons they had in grammar and syntax. This horror is quite justified. We should not conclude from this, however, that the learning of grammar is useless as such and ought to be done away with. This would be an utterly false idea. In seeking to find what is right by going from one extreme to the other it might be natural enough to come up with the suggestion: Let us do away with grammar; let's teach the children to read by the practical method of selecting passages for them, let us teach them to read and write without any grammar! This idea could arise quite easily out of the horror that so many of us remember. But learning grammar is not an unnecessary factor, especially not in our day and age, for the following reason.

What is it we do when we raise unconscious speech to the grammatical realm, to the knowledge of grammar? We make the transition with our pupils of lifting speech from the unconscious into the conscious realm; our purpose is not to teach them grammar in a pedantic way but to raise something to consciousness that otherwise takes place unconsciously. Unconsciously or semi-consciously man does indeed use the world as a trellis up which to climb in a manner that corresponds to what we learn in grammar. Grammar tells us, for instance, that there are nouns. Nouns are names for objects, for objects that in a sense are self-contained in space. That we meet such objects in life is not without significance for this life of ours. All things that can be expressed by nouns awaken our consciousness to our independence as human beings. By learning to name things with nouns we distinguish ourselves from the world around us. By calling a thing a table or a chair we separate ourselves from the table or chair: we are here, the table or chair is there. It is quite another matter to describe things with adjectives. When I say: The chair is blue—I am expressing something that unites me with the chair. The characteristic that I perceive unites me with the chair. By naming something with a noun I dissociate myself from it; when I describe it with an adjective I become one with it again. Thus the development of our consciousness takes place in our relationship to things when we address them; we must certainly become conscious of the way we address them. If I say the verb: the man writes—I not only unite myself with the being about whom I have spoken the verb, I also do with him what he is doing in his physical body. I do what he does, my ego does what he does. When I speak a verb my ego joins in with what the physical body of the other person is doing. I unite my ego with the physical body of the other when I speak a verb. Our listening, especially with verbs, is in reality always a participation. What is so far the most spiritual part of man participates, only it suppresses the activity. Only in eurythmy is this activity placed in the external world. In addition to everything else, eurythmy also gives the activity of listening. When one person tells something, the other listens; he performs in his ego what lives physically in the sounds, but he suppresses it. The ego always does eurythmy in participation, and what eurythmy puts before us through the physical body is nothing other than a making visible of listening. So you always do eurythmy when you listen, and when you actually do eurythmy you are just making visible what you leave invisible when you listen. The manifestation of the activity of the listening human being is in fact eurythmy. It is not something arbitrary but rather in reality the revelation of what the listening human being does. People are of course today fearfully slovenly in themselves, so at first when they listen they do some fearfully bad inner eurythmy. By doing it as it should be done they raise it till it becomes real eurythmy. Through eurythmy people will learn to listen properly, for nowadays they cannot listen properly. I have made some curious discoveries during my recent lectures.[20] Speakers come forward during the discussion, but from what they say one notices quite soon that they have really not heard the lecture at all, not even physically, but have only heard certain parts of it. This is enormously significant, particularly in the present epoch of our human development. So someone or other enters into the discussion and speaks of whatever he has been used to thinking for decades. You find yourself speaking in front of people with socialist ideas but they only hear what they have been hearing from their activists for decades; the rest they do not hear at all, not even physically. They sometimes quite innocently admit as much by saying: Dr. Steiner says a lot of good things, but he doesn't say anything new!—People have become so rigid from their listening that they confuse everything that has not been fossilized within them for decades. People cannot listen and will become increasingly less able to do so in our age unless the power of listening is reawakened by eurythmy.

The soul being of man must find some healing again. Therefore it will be particularly important in school to add another factor to the hygiene of the body provided by gymnastics and to everything that takes account only of the physiology of bodily functions. This other factor is a hygiene of the soul, and this requires that gymnastics lessons should alternate with eurythmy lessons. Though eurythmy is primarily an art, nevertheless its health-giving forces will be specially beneficial to the pupils, for in eurythmy they will learn not only something artistic; through eurythmy they will learn the same for their soul as they learn through gymnastics for their body, and the way these two things work into one another will be very fine. It is essential to educate our children in a way that will enable them to notice once again the world around them and their fellow men. This is of course the foundation of all social life. Everyone talks today of social impulses, yet none but anti-social urges are to be found among men. Socialism ought to have its roots in the new esteem men should gain for one another. But there can only be mutual esteem when people really listen to each other. If we are to become teachers and educators it will be vastly important that we turn our sensitivity to these things once more.

Now that you know that when you speak a noun you dissociate yourself from your environment, that when you speak an adjective you unite yourself with your surroundings, and that when you speak a verb you blossom out into your environment, you move with it, now that you know all this you will speak with quite a different inner emphasis about the noun, the adjective and the verb than would be the case if you did not have this consciousness. However, all this is still only a preliminary and is to be continued. At this moment, though, I only want to evoke certain ideas whose absence might confuse you.

It is, then, extraordinarily important for us to know what it means for man to become conscious of the structure of language. In addition to this we must develop a feeling for the great wisdom in language. This feeling, too, has all but died out today. Language is far cleverer than any of us. You will surely believe me when I say that the structure of language has not been built by human beings. Just imagine what would have been the result if people had sat in parliaments in order in their cleverness to decree the structure of language! Something about as clever as our laws! The structure of language, however, is truly cleverer than our statutory laws. Inherent in the structure of language is the greatest wisdom. And an extraordinary amount can be learnt from the way a people or a tribe speaks. Entering consciously in a living way into the framework of language we can learn a very great deal from the genius of language itself. It is of the utmost importance to learn to feel something concrete of the working and weaving of the spirits of language. To believe that the genius of language works in the structure of language is of great significance. This feeling can be extended further to the point where we realize: We human beings speak; animals cannot yet speak; they have at most the beginnings of articulated speech.—In our day and age, when people like to obliterate everything, speech is even ascribed to ants and bees. But in the light of reality this is nonsense. It is all built on a form of judgment to which I have frequently drawn attention. There are some natural philosophers today who consider themselves most wise and say: Why should not plants, too, have a will life and a feeling life? Are there not plants, the so-called carnivorous plants, that attract small animals that fly near them and then snap shut on them when they have settled?—So these are beings that seem to have a will relationship with whatever comes into their vicinity. But we cannot claim that such outward signs are really characteristics of will. When I meet this attitude of mind I usually say, using the same form of logic: I know of something that also waits till a live creature comes near it and then encloses and imprisons it; a mousetrap.—The mere appearance of a mousetrap might therefore just as well be taken as proof of its possessing life as that of the Venus's flytrap as proof that it possesses consciousness.

We must be profoundly conscious that the power of articulate speech is a human possession. And we must also be conscious of our position in the world over against the other three kingdoms of nature. When we are conscious of this we also know that our ego is very much bound up with everything that constitutes speech, though today's speaking has become very abstract for us. But I would like to remind you of something from which you can win a new respect for language. In ancient times, for instance in the Jewish culture—though it was yet more pronounced in the even older epochs—the priests or those whose task it was to administer and represent the cult would, during the celebration of the rites, cease speaking when they came to certain concepts. They interrupted their speech and conveyed the names of high beings not in words but in silence with suitable eurythmic gestures. Then they would continue with the spoken rites. Thus for instance the name that sounds so abstract to us, rendered in Hebrew by 'I AM the I AM', was never uttered. The priest spoke up to the point where it occurred, then he made the gesture, and then he resumed his speech. What he expressed in his gesture was 'the unutterable name of God in man'. Why was this done? It was done because if this name had been spoken and repeated without more ado, people in the state of sensitivity that was theirs at that time would have been stunned. There were sounds and combinations of sounds in speech that could stun the people of those ancient cultures, so great was their effect upon them. Something akin to fainting would have come over the people if such words had been spoken and heard. That is why they spoke of the 'unutterable name of God'. This was profoundly significant. You find this described when it is said: Such names may only be spoken by the priests and even by them only on special occasions, for were they to be spoken before unprepared hearers, heaven and earth would collapse. This means that people would fall unconscious. Therefore such a name was expressed only in a gesture. Such a feeling is an expression of what speech really is. Today people thoughtlessly blurt out everything. We can no longer vary the feeling nuances and it is very rare to find a person who can be moved enough, without being sentimental, to have tears in his eyes for instance when he comes across certain passages in a novel. This is today something quite atavistic. The lively feeling for what lies in speech and sensitivity to language has become very dulled.

This is one of the many things that need to be quickened again today and it is something, when we do enliven it, that will enable us to feel more clearly what we really have in speech. We have speech to thank for much that lives in our feeling of egohood, in our feeling of being a personality. Our feelings can rise to a mood almost of prayer: I hear the language around me being spoken and through the speech the power of ego flows into me!—Once you have this feeling for the sanctity of the summoning of the ego through speech you will be able to awaken it also in the children by a variety of means. Then, too, you will awaken the feeling of egohood in the children not in an egoistic manner but in another way. For there are two ways of awakening the feeling of egohood in the child. Done wrongly it serves to fan the flames of egoism; done rightly it stimulates the will, in fact real selflessness and willingness to live with the outer world.

What I have now said is spoken to you because as teachers and educators you must be permeated by it. It will be for you to use it in teaching language and speech. We shall speak tomorrow of how we can in practice permeate it with consciousness in order to awaken in the children the sense for consciousness of personality.

LECTURE FIVE

Stuttgart, 26 August 1919

Yesterday we discussed how the first lesson in school should begin. Obviously I cannot go on to describe every single step, but I should like to indicate the essential course the lessons should take in a way that will enable you in practice to make something of what I say.

You saw that we attached the greatest importance to making the children first of all aware of the reason for coming to school; then they had to be made aware that they have hands. When they have become conscious of this we should start with some drawing and even make the transition to painting through which a sense for what is beautiful and less beautiful can be developed. We saw that this emerging sense can also be observed in hearing and that the first elements of a musical sense for what is beautiful and less beautiful will follow from this.

Let us now turn to the next step. We shall assume that you have continued for a while in the exercises with crayons and paints. If what is learnt is to be built on good foundations it is essential that learning to write should be preceded by some concentration on drawing so that writing can to some extent be derived from drawing. It is furthermore essential that the reading of print should be derived from the reading of handwriting. Thus we shall endeavour to find the transition from drawing to writing, from writing to reading handwriting and from reading handwriting to reading print. Let us now assume that you have reached the stage of letting the children find their feet in drawing so that they have mastered to some extent the making of the curved and straight forms that will be needed in writing. We now seek the transition to what we have already described as the basis for writing and reading lessons. Today I shall start with a few examples of how you might proceed.

We assume, then, that the children have reached the point where they can master straight and curved lines with their little hands. You then endeavour to show them that there are such things as letters, a whole lot of them. We started with the fish and F. The sequence you follow is quite immaterial and you need not proceed in alphabetical order; I shall do so now merely so that you have some sort of comprehensive record. Let us see what success we have in proceeding to evolve writing and reading out of your own free imagination. I would now say to the children: You know what a bath is.—(Let me here interpolate another point: It is very important in teaching to be cunning in a rational manner, that is always to have something up your sleeve that can contribute unseen to the children's education. In this sense it is good to use the word *bath* for the step I am about to describe, so that now they are in school the children are reminded of a bath, of washing themselves, of cleanliness as such. It is good always to have something like this in the background without actually mentioning it or concealing it in admonishments. It is good to choose examples that compel the children to think of something which might also contribute to a moral and aesthetic attitude.) Then you continue: You see, when grown-ups want to write down what a bath is they do it like this, *bath*. This is the picture of what you express when you say *bath*, when you mean a bath.—Now I again let a number of the children copy this, just copy it, so that whenever they are given something like this it also goes straight into their hands, so that they take it in not just by looking but with their whole being. Then I say: Watch how you start to say *bath*; let us look at the beginning of *bath*, B.—The children have to be led from saying the whole word *bath* to just breathing the initial sound, as I illustrated with the fish. The next thing to make clear to them is that just as *bath* is the sign for the whole bath, so B is the sign for the beginning of the word *bath*.

Then I explain that a beginning like this can also be found in other words. I say: If you say *band* you also start like this; if you say *bow*, like the bow some people wear in their hair, you again start in the same way. Have you ever seen a bear in the zoo? When you start to say *bear* you again breathe the same sound. All these words start with the same sound.—Thus I endeavour to lead the child from the whole word to the beginning of the word, finding the transition to the single sound or letter, always finding the initial letter from the whole word.

It is important that you yourselves should perhaps try to develop the initial letter in a meaningful way out of the drawing element. You will manage this very well if you simply use your imagination and say to yourselves: The people who first saw such animals as those that begin with B, like beavers and bears, they drew the animal's back, its hind paws standing on the ground and its forepaws lifted up; they drew an animal in the act of rising on to its hind legs and their drawing turned into a B. You will always find that the initial letter of a word is a drawing, an animal or

plant form or some external object; you can give your imagination free reign and there is no need to delve into cultural histories which are anyway incomplete. Historically the fact is that if you go back to the most ancient forms of Egyptian writing, which was still a sign writing, you find a great many copies of objects and animals in the letters. Not till the transition from the Egyptian to the Phoenician culture did the change take place that brought with it the development of the picture into a sign representing a sound. It is this transition that the children must experience over again. Let us therefore gain a clear idea of it ourselves in theory.

When writing first began to develop in ancient Egypt, every detail that was to be written down was written in picture writing; it was drawn, although the drawing had to be as simplified as possible. If somebody employed in copying this picture writing made a mistake, if for instance a holy word was misrepresented by him, the scribe was condemned to death. We see thus how very, very seriously anything connected with writing was taken in ancient Egypt. All writing at that time consisted of pictures of the kind described. Then cultural life was taken up by the Phoenicians who lived more firmly in the external world. By them the initial picture of a word was retained and transferred to represent the sound. Since we are not here to study Egyptian languages, let me give you an example that is also valid for Egyptian and is most easily adapted in our own language. The Egyptians knew that the sound M could be depicted by watching mainly the upper lip. They therefore took the sign for M from the picture of the upper lip. From this sign the letter emerged that we use for the beginning of the word *mouth*, the letter that is also valid for any other word beginning with this sound. In this way the picture sign for a word became the sign for a sound because the picture for the beginning of the word was used.

This principle, having been adhered to in the history of writing and its development, is also excellent as a principle to be used in teaching and we shall use it here. That is, we shall endeavour to arrive at letters by starting with drawings: Just as from the fish with its two fins we arrived at the F, so do we move from the bear dancing on its hind legs to the B; from the upper lip we come to the mouth and from the mouth to the M; with our imagination we seek to pave the way for the child from drawing to writing. I told you it was unnecessary to make extensive studies of the history of writing in order to find what you need. What you might

discover through such studies would serve you far less in your teaching than what you will find through your own activity of soul and your own imagination. The kind of activity necessary for the study of the history of writing would make you so dead that you would have a far less living influence on your pupils than would be the case if you yourself arrive at the idea of deriving the B from the bear. Working things out for yourself in this way will refresh you so much that what you want to tell your pupils will have a far more living effect than would be the case if you were to seek material for your lessons by making historical researches. Looking at life and your teaching with regard to these two aspects, you must ask: What is more important? To take in an historical fact with great effort and then strenuously seek to weave it into your lessons, or to have such agility of soul that you can invent your own examples to offer to your pupils with your own enthusiasm? It will always give you joy, albeit a quiet joy, to transfer to a letter the shape you have yourself made out of some animal or plant. And this joy that you yourself have will live in what you make out of your pupil.

Next we point out to the children that what they have found at the beginning of a word can also appear in the middle. You say, for instance: You have all seen a little baby; when grown-ups want to write the word *baby* they do it like this, *baby*. Here you can see what you had at the beginning in *bear* is now at the beginning and in the middle in *baby*.* You always use capital letters to start with so that the children recognize the similarity with the picture. In this way you teach them that what they have learnt in connection with the beginning of a word can also be found in the middle of a word. This is another step in the process of dividing the whole into parts for them.

You see how the important thing for us in our endeavour to achieve teaching that is living rather than dead is always to start from the whole. Just as in arithmetic we start not from the addenda but from the sum which we divide into parts, so here too we proceed from the whole to the parts. The great advantage gained from this in teaching and education is that we are thus able to place the child in the world in a living way; for the world is a totality and the child maintains permanent links with the living whole if we proceed in the way I have indicated. If you let him learn the individual letters from the picture, this gives him a link with living reality. But you must never neglect to write the letter forms so that they are seen to arise from the picture,

* Translator's note: Rudolf Steiner used the German word *Rebe* (vine) as his example here, so I have freely adapted his meaning to an English word.

and you must always take into account that the consonants are explained as pictures of external objects but never the vowels. Your point of departure for the vowels is that they always render man's inner being and his relationship to the external world. For example, when you are teaching the children the letter A (Tr. note: corresponding to 'a' in father) you will say to them: Think of the sun that you see in the morning. Can any of you remember what you did when the sun rose this morning?—Perhaps one or other of the children will remember what they did. If none of them remembers, they will have to be helped to recall how they must have stood there and how if the sunrise was very beautiful they must have said: Ah! It is a note of feeling that must be struck; the resonance that sounds in the vowel must be called forth from the feeling. Then you must try to say: When you stood like that and said *Ah* it was just as if from your inner being a beam of sunlight spread out from

your mouth. What lives in you when you see the sunrise comes out of you and streams forth (see left-hand drawing) when you say *Ah*. But you do not let all of it stream out, you keep some of it back and then it becomes this sign.—(See right-hand drawing.) You should try once to clothe with a drawing what lies in the breath when a vowel is spoken. In this way you will find drawings that can show you in a picture how the signs for the vowels have come about. Primitive cultures do not have many vowels, not even the primitive cultures of today. The languages of primitive cultures are very rich in consonants; these people can express many more things in consonants than we know how to. They even click their tongues and are skilled in articulating all sorts of complicated consonants with in between only a hint of vowel sounds. You will find sounds made by African tribesmen that resemble the crack of a whip and so on, while the vowels are only faintly heard. The European travellers who meet these tribes usually sound their vowels much more strongly than the tribesmen do.

So we can always evolve the vowels out of drawing. For instance by appealing to the children's feelings you can try

to make them imagine themselves in the following situation: Think what would happen if your brother or sister were to come to you and say something you did not straight away understand. After a while you begin to understand what they mean. Then what do you say?—One of the children may answer or you may have to point out to them that they would say: *Eee* (Tr. note: rendered in German by the letter I). The shape of the sound *eee* when it is drawn contains a pointing towards whatever has been understood, indeed it is a rather rough expression of pointing to something. In eurythmy you find it expressed very clearly. So a simple line becomes an 'I', a simple line that ought to be fatter at the bottom and thinner at the top, only instead of that we make a line and express the thinner part with a smaller sign above it. In this way every vowel can be derived out of the shape of the aspiration, of the breath.

By this method you will succeed in teaching the children at first a kind of sign writing. You need not be at all shy of calling to your aid certain ideas that arouse in the feeling life something that really did live in the process of cultural development. You could thus teach the children the following. You could say: Have you ever seen a tall building with a dome on top?* A dome, D. But then you would have to make the D like this: ⌂. But this was awkward, so people upended it and made D. Such ideas really are inherent in writing and you can certainly make use of them: After a while people did not want their writing to be so complicated, they wanted it to be simpler. So out of this sign D,

which really ought to be ⌂, they made (now you proceed to the small letters) this sign, the small d. You can most certainly evolve the existing letter shapes in this way out of such figures that you have taught the children in drawing. By always pointing out the transition from form to form and never teaching in an abstract way you help the children to progress so that they can find the genuine transition from the form derived at first from the drawing to the shape the letter really has today in handwriting.

There are some individuals today, though they are few and far between, who have recognized such things. There are educationists who have pointed out that writing ought to be derived from drawing. Yet they proceed in a different manner from that required here. Their starting point is the shape of the letters as they are today, so instead of proceeding from the sign for the dancing bear to the B they take the B and carve it up into separate lines and curves: **| ⊃** and seek in this way to lead the children from drawing to writing. They advocate an abstract version of what we are

* Translator's note: Rudolf Steiner's example here is *Dach* (roof) Dome fits the letter D so well that I have used it here and only very slightly altered the text accordingly.

trying to do quite concretely. These educationists are quite right in seeing that it would be practical to proceed from drawing to writing, but people today are too entangled in the dead wood of our culture to hit upon a clearly living way of going about things.

Let me not forget to warn you at this point against being taken in by all sorts of modern endeavours that might tempt you to say: Here efforts are being made to do this and there efforts are being made to do that. For you will always discover that the intentions have no very deep foundations. Somehow people are constantly impelled to attempt such things. But they will not succeed in achieving them until mankind has accepted spiritual science as a part of culture.

So we can always make a connection with man and his relation to the world around him by teaching writing in an organic way and by teaching reading by starting with the reading of handwriting.

Now it is natural to teaching—and we should not leave this out of account—that there is a certain yearning for complete freedom. Notice how freedom flows into this discussion of how we might prepare ourselves to be teachers. Our discussion has inwardly something to do with freedom. For I have pointed out to you that you should not make yourselves unfree by toiling away at the study of how writing came into being during the transition from Egyptian to Phoenician culture; what you have to do is yourselves develop your own soul capacities. What can be done by this method will of course differ from teacher to teacher. Not everyone can use a dancing bear; someone might use something much better for the same purpose. The final result, though, can be achieved just as well by one teacher as another. Every individual gives of himself when he teaches. In this his freedom remains inviolate. The more the teachers desire to preserve their freedom in this respect, the more they will be able to enter into their teaching by giving of themselves. This is something that has been almost entirely lost in recent times, as you can see from a certain phenomenon.

Some time ago (the younger among you may not remember the matter but it caused the older ones, who knew what it entailed, a good deal of annoyance) preparations were made to do something in the cultural sphere that very much resembled the introduction of the notorious Imperial German State Gravy in the material sphere. You know how it has often been stressed that there ought to be a standard sauce or gravy for all inns that do not have to reckon with an elite foreign clientele but serve only Germans. Well, just as this Imperial German State Gravy was to be. standardized, so now spelling, orthography, was to be standardized. Now people have the most curious attitude to this question and there are concrete examples demonstrating this. There is in German literature an instance of a most beautiful, tender relationship, that between Novalis[21] and a certain lady. This relationship is so beautiful because when the lady in question had passed away, Novalis continued quite consciously to live with her when she was already in the spiritual world, following her through death in an inner meditative activity of soul. Of this he spoke. This relationship between Novalis and his beloved is one of the most entrancing and intimate episodes in the history of German literature. Now there exists a highly intelligent (and seen from its own point of view also interesting) strictly philological treatise by a German scholar on this relationship between Novalis and the lady. This delicate, tender relationship is 'put in its proper light' through the proof that this lady died before she had learnt to spell properly. She made spelling mistakes in her letters! In short, we are given (with the strictest scientific accuracy of course) a thoroughly banal picture of this person who had such a special relationship with Novalis. This scientific method is so good that any dissertation made in accordance with it would earn the highest marks! I only want to remind you that people seem to have forgotten that Goethe was never able to spell properly, that all through his life he made spelling mistakes, particularly when he was young. Yet despite this he rose to Goethean greatness! Not to mention the people he knew and thought highly of: their letters, nowadays sometimes published in facsimile, would earn nothing but red corrections from the hand of a schoolmaster! They would get thoroughly poor marks!

All this is linked to a rather unfree aspect of our life, an aspect that ought to play no part in teaching and education. But a few decades ago it was so pronounced that it infuriated the more enlightened teachers. Standard German spelling was to be introduced, the famous Puttkammer orthography. This meant that the state not only exercised the right of supervision and administration in schools but actually laid down the law on spelling. The result is just what you might expect! For this Puttkammer spelling system has robbed us of much that might still have revealed something of the more intimate aspects of the German language. Seeing only the abstract spelling of today, people have lost much in written German of what used to live in the German language.

What matters most in such things is the right attitude of mind. Obviously we cannot let spelling run riot but we can at least recognize what the opposite points of view are. If, once people had learnt to write, they were allowed to put down what they heard either from others or from themselves just as they heard it, their spelling would be very varied, very individualized. This would be extraordinarily interesting but it would make communication more difficult. On the other hand our task is to develop not only our own individuality in community with others but also our social impulses and feelings. In this, a great deal of what could be revealed as our own individuality is rubbed off in what we have to develop for the sake of living together with others. We should feel that this is so, we should be taught to feel that we do such a thing purely for social reasons. Therefore when you begin to orient your writing lessons towards spelling, your starting point must be a quite specific set of feelings. You will again and again have to point out to the children (as I have already said in another connection) that they should respect and esteem the grown-ups, that they are themselves growing up into a world that is already formed and waiting to receive them, and that therefore they must take notice of what is already there. This is the point of view from which the children must be introduced to things like correct spelling. Spelling lessons must run parallel with developing their feeling of respect and esteem for what their predecessors have established. Spelling must not be taught as an abstraction as though it existed as an absolute on the basis of some divine—or shall we say Puttkammer—law or other; you must develop in the children the feeling: the grown-ups whom we are to respect spell like this, so we ought to follow their example. From this will result a certain variability in spelling, but it will not be excessive; there will be a certain adaptation of the growing child to the world of the grown-ups. And we must count on this adaptation. It is not our task to create in him the belief: this is right, this is wrong. The only belief we should arouse, thus building on living authority, is: this is the way the grown-ups do it.

This is what I meant when I said that we must find the transition from the child's first period up to the change of teeth to his second period up to puberty by making the transition from the principle of imitation to that of authority. What I mean by this must be introduced everywhere in practice not by drilling the children to respect authority but by acting in a way that will help their feeling for authority to arise, for instance by teaching spelling in a way that places it on a foundation of authority in the way I have just described.

LECTURE SIX

Stuttgart, 27 August 1919

You will have to be not only teachers at the Waldorf School but also, if things turn out as they should, advocates of the whole Waldorf school system. For you will know the real purpose of the Waldorf School far more clearly than anything that can be put over either to the more immediate or the wider public. And so that you can in the right sense be advocates of what is striven for with the Waldorf School and with it for cultural life in general, you will have to be in a position to defend it even against public opinions that are antagonistic or merely disapproving. Consequently I must include in our discussions of teaching methods a chapter that actually follows quite naturally from what we have been discussing so far in these sessions.

You know that in the field of education, as well as elsewhere, great things are expected nowadays of so-called experimental psychology. Experiments are carried out on people to determine what constitutes an individual's ability to form concepts, or to memorize, or even how his will functions, though naturally the latter can only be done in a roundabout way since the will is a process that occurs in a state of sleep. In the same way what people experience in sleep can only be indirectly determined by means of electrical equipment in the laboratory and not by direct observation. Well, such experiments are made. Please do not think that I am wholly against such experiments. They can be meaningful as feelers of science probing new fields like tendrils. A great many interesting things can be discovered by means of experimentation and I certainly do not want to condemn them wholesale. I would be only too pleased if everyone wanting to could have access to a psychological laboratory in which to conduct experiments. We must consider for a moment the rise of this experimental psychology, particularly in the form recommended by the educationist *Meumann*[22] who basically belongs to the Herbartian school.

Why is experimental psychology practised today? Because people have lost the gift of observing man directly. They can no longer rely on the forces that link, inwardly link man to man and thus also man to child. Therefore they seek to find out by external means how to treat the growing child. You see how much more inward is the path we want to follow in our education and our teaching methods. This path is urgently needed for the present and also for the near future of mankind. On the one hand we see the growth of this urge towards experimental psychology, and on the other hand we also see how these very methods lead to a misconception of certain simple facts of life. Let me illustrate this by an example.

Experimental psychologists have recently been particularly interested in what they call the process of comprehension, for instance the process of comprehension in reading, in the reading of a given passage. In order to determine what the process of comprehension is they have tried to work with people whom they designate 'experimental subjects'. Put briefly, the very lengthy experiments take the following course. An experimental subject, a child or an older person, is presented with a reading passage, and investigations are then made into what the child, for instance, should most profitably do first in order to achieve the most rapid comprehension. It is noted that the most expedient method is first to introduce the person to the subject matter of the passage. A further series of experiments show that the experimental subject then carries out a process of 'passive assimilation'. So after the content has been introduced it is then passively assimilated. Out of this passive assimilation of a reading passage is supposed to arise the faculty of 'anticipatory learning', the ability to reproduce what was first introduced and then passively assimilated in a free spiritual activity. And the fourth act of this drama is then the recapitulation of all the points that are still uncertain, in other words that have not entered fully into the person's life of soul and spirit. So if you let the experimental subject carry out in proper sequence first the process of becoming acquainted with the content of the passage, then the process of passive assimilation, then the process of anticipatory learning and finally the process of recapitulating whatever is not fully understood, you will come to the conclusion that this is the most expedient method of assimilating, reading and retaining something that is to be read. Do not misunderstand me: I am putting this forward because I must, in view of the fact that people talk at cross-purposes so much these days; it is possible to want to express an identical point with diametrically opposed words. Accordingly the experimental psychologists will maintain that by such painstaking methods we can learn what we ought to be doing in education. But those who recognize more deeply the life of the human being as a whole know that you cannot arrive at a real educational activity by these means any more than you can put together a live beetle after you have dissected it. This is just not possible. It is equally impossible when you anatomize the human being's soul activity. Of course it is interesting and can in other connections also be most fruitful to carry out anatomy of human soul activity. But it does not make teachers! Therefore this experimental psychology will not in fact lead to a re-establishment of education; this can only arise out of an inner understanding of man.

I had to say this lest you should misunderstand a statement I now want to make, a statement that will very much irritate those who are attached to the present-day climate of opinion. The statement is naturally one-sided in the way I shall put it, and its one-sidedness must, of course, be counterbalanced. What do the experimental psychologists discover when they have anatomized, or should we say tortured (for the procedure is not pleasant) the soul of their experimental subject? They have discovered what is in their opinion an extraordinarily significant result that appears written large again and again in educational handbooks as a final conclusion. Put in clear language, the result, roughly, is: that a passage to be read and learnt is more easily retained if the content is understood than if it is not understood. To use the scientific idiom, 'it has been determined by research' that it is expedient first to discover the meaning of a passage, for then the passage is easier to learn. Now I must make my heretical statement: If the conclusion of these experiments is correct, then I could have known it anyway, for I should like to know what person equipped with ordinary common sense would not already realize that a passage is easier to remember if you have understood the sense of it than if you have not. There is no doubt about it that results of experimental psychology bring to light the most terribly obvious truths. The truisms you find in the textbooks of experimental psychology are on occasion such that no one who has not trained himself in the pursuit of science to accept the fascinating along with the absolutely tedious could possibly bring himself to bother with them. People do, in fact, become inured to this kind of thing even by the way they are drilled in their early school days, for the phenomenon is present already there, though less pronounced by far than in the universities.

This heretical statement, namely that it is rather obvious that you have to know the meaning of something that you are supposed to remember, is aimed particularly at teachers.

But there is something else to consider: What is assimilated as meaning only works on the faculty of observation, the faculty of cognizing through thought; by laying emphasis on the meaning we educate a person onesidedly merely to observe the world, to know it through thought. So if we were to teach only in accordance with that statement the result would be nothing but weak-willed individuals. Therefore the statement is right in a way and yet not entirely correct. To be absolutely correct we should have to say: If you want to do the best you can for an individual's faculty of cognizing through thought, you will have to analyse the meaning of everything that he is to take in and retain. It is indeed a fact that by first onesidedly analysing the meaning of everything we can go a long way in the education of man's observation of the world. But we would get nowhere in educating his will, for we cannot force the will to emerge by throwing a strong light on the meaning of anything. The will wants to sleep, it does not want to be awakened fully by what I might call the perpetual unchaste laying bare of meaning. Thus it is simply a necessity of life that penetrates beyond the simple truth about the revelation of meaning and gives rise to the fact that we must also do things with the children that do not call for the laying bare of meaning. Then we shall educate their will.

The unseemly practice of onesidedly using the revelation of meaning has run riot particularly in movements like the Theosophical Movement. You know how much I have protested over the years against a certain bad habit in theosophical circles. I have even had to see *Hamlet*, a pure work of art, explained in theosophical jargon: This is manas, that is the ego, there is the astral body; one character is one thing, another something else. Explanations of this kind were particularly favoured. I have fulminated against this sort of thing because it is a sin against human life to interpret symbolically something that is meant to be directly taken in as pure art. A meaning is thus read into things in an unseemly fashion that raises them up as objects of mere observation to a position they ought not to occupy. All this stems from the fact that the Theosophical Movement is a decadent movement. It is the ultimate remnant of a declining culture, not something that has in its whole attitude anything to do with Anthroposophy. This Anthroposophy aims at being the opposite: an ascending movement, the beginning of an ascent. This is radically different. That is why in the theosophical realm so much comes to the fore that is fundamentally a manifestation of extreme decadence. But that there are people at all who can actually perpetrate the symbolical interpretation of the different characters in *Hamlet* is the consequence of the atrocious education we have had and of the way we have striven to be educated only in the realm of meaning.

Human life calls for more than education in the realm of meaning, it calls for education in what the will experiences in its sleeping condition: rhythm, beat, melody, the harmony of colours, repetition, any kind of activity not calling for a grasp of meaning. If you let the child repeat sentences that he is nowhere near to understanding because he is too young, if you make him learn these sentences by heart, you are not working on his faculty of understanding since you cannot explain the meaning which will only emerge later on for him, you are working on his will, and that is what you should, indeed you must, do. You must on the one hand endeavour to bring to the child whatever is pre-eminently artistic: music, drawing, modelling and so on; but on the other hand you must bring to the child things that have an abstract meaning in such a way that though he cannot understand the meaning as yet, he will be able to do so later on when he is more mature because he has taken them in through repetition and can remember them. If you have done this, you have worked on his will. And quite especially

you have also worked on his feeling life, and that is something you should not forget. Just as feeling—and this is
revealed both from the point of view of the soul and of the
spirit—lies between willing and thinking, so do the educational measures for the feeling life lie between those for the
faculty of cognizing through thought and those for the will
and its development. For thinking and knowing we must
certainly undertake measures that involve the revelation of
meaning: reading, writing and so on. For willed activity we
must cultivate everything that does not involve just the
interpretation of meaning but requires to be directly
grasped by the whole human being: everything artistic.
What lies between these two will work in the main on the
development of the feeling life, of the heart forces. These
heart forces are indeed strongly affected if the child is given
the opportunity of first learning something by rote without
understanding it and without any explanations of the meaning, though of course there is a meaning, and if he then
later, when he has matured through other processes, remembers what he has learnt and now understands what he took
into himself earlier. This subtle process must be very much
taken into account in teaching if we want to bring up
human beings who have an inward life of feeling. For feeling
establishes itself in life in a peculiar manner. People ought to
observe what goes on in this realm. But they do not do so
effectively. Let me suggest to you an observation that you
can easily make with a little effort.

Suppose you wanted to obtain a clear picture of the state
of Goethe's soul in 1790. You can do so by studying just a
selection of the things he produced during that year. There
is a chronological list of all his poems at the end of every
edition of his works. So you ponder on the poems he wrote
in 1790 and on whatever plays he created. You call to mind
that he finished his beautiful treatise on *The Metamorphosis of
Plants* during that year and you remember that he for-

mulated the first ideas about his *Theory of Colours*. Out of all
this you form a picture of his mood of soul in 1790 and ask:
What played into this soul life of Goethe in 1790? You will
find the answer to this question only if you cast a searching
look over everything that happened to Goethe from 1749 to
1790 and over everything that followed on—which Goethe
did not know then but you know now—from that year until
his death in 1832. The remarkable realization emerges that
Goethe's state of soul in 1790 was a combination of what
was to come later, what still had to be achieved, and what
had gone before, what had already been experienced. This
is an extraordinarily significant observation. But people shy
away from it because it leads to realms that they understand-
ably do not like impinging on for such observations. Try
yourselves to observe in this way the soul life of a person
whom you knew for some time who has recently died. If you
train yourselves to a more subtle observation of the soul you
will discover the following. Somebody who was your friend
died, let us say in 1918. You have known the person for some
time, so that you can ask: What was his state of soul in
1912? Taking everything into account that you know of
him, you will find that his soul mood in 1912 already had
unconsciously playing into it the preparation for the death
he was soon to meet; it played unconsciously into his feeling
life at that time. The feeling life in its totality is what I call
the mood of soul. A person who is soon to die has quite a
different mood of soul from one who still has long to live.

Now you will understand why people are not eager to
make such observations, for to put it mildly, it would be
rather uncomfortable to observe a person's imminent death
expressed in his soul mood. And it is indeed expressed
there. But for ordinary life it is not good that people should
notice such things. That is why on the whole it is removed
from ordinary life rather as the will as a sleeping force is
removed from waking consiousness even when we are

awake. But the teacher must, after all, take up a position outside ordinary life to some extent. He must not shrink from standing outside this ordinary life and accepting truths for the sake of his work that may bring a shocking or tragic element to ordinary life. There is some lost ground to be recovered in this respect, especially in the educational system of Central Europe. You know how during the earlier decades of this Central European educational life teachers, especially in the grammar schools and lycées, were still people who were rather looked down upon by the ordinary man of the world. Unworldly, pedantic fellows who did not know how to behave properly in society, always wore long frock-coats instead of dinner jackets and so on; these were at one time the teachers of young people, especially the more mature youngsters. Recently things have changed. University professors have begun to wear proper dinner jackets and even manage to cope quite well with the world, and the fact that the former state of affairs has been overcome is regarded as a great step forward. This is a good thing. But it also needs to be overcome in another direction. In future this state of affairs must also be overcome in the sense that the way a teacher stands outside life must not consist merely in always appearing in a long frock-coat when other people are wearing dinner jackets. He may in a way retain his position of being somewhat outside life, but this should be linked with a deeper view of life than can be achieved by those who wear dinner jackets for certain occasions. I am speaking only figuratively, of course, for I have nothing against dinner jackets.

A teacher must be able to regard life more profoundly, otherwise he will never succeed in handling the growing human being in an appropriate and fruitful manner. Therefore he will have to accept certain truths like the one I have just mentioned. Life itself demands in a sense that it shall contain secrets. It is not diplomatic secrets that we

need for the immediate future. What we need for education
is a knowledge of certain mysteries of life. The ancient
teachers of the Mysteries used to preserve such secrets as
esoteric knowledge because they could not be given over
directly to life. And in a certain sense every teacher must be
in possession of truths that he cannot directly pass on to the
world, for the world that lives outside and does not have the
task of educating the young would be confused in its healthy
progress if it had daily access to such truths. You do not
understand fully how to treat the growing child if you are
unable to discern what path something takes within him
when you tell it to him in a way that he cannot fully
understand at his present stage of development, but that he
will understand later when you come back to it again and
are then able to explain to him not only what you now tell
him but also what he took into himself earlier. This works
very strongly on the heart forces. That is why it is so
essential in any good school that for as long as at all possible
the teacher should remain with his group of pupils: He takes
them on in the first class, continues with them in the
following year in the second class, moves on again with
them to the third class and so on as far as external circumstances will allow. And the teacher who has had the eighth
class this year should start again with the first class in the
following year. For it is sometimes only appropriate to
return years later to something you have instilled into the
children's souls. Whatever the circumstances, the education
of the heart forces suffers if the children have a new teacher
each year who cannot follow up what has been instilled into
their souls in previous years. It is a part of teaching method
that the teacher moves up through the school with his
pupils. Only if this is done can one work with the rhythms of
life. And life has a rhythm in the most comprehensive sense.
This is apparent in day to day life in the tasks we set about.
If, for instance, you have become accustomed over the

period of just one week to eating a roll and butter at half past ten every morning, you will probably find that you are quite hungry for your buttered roll at the same time in the second week. So easily does the human organism adapt to a rhythm. And not only the external organism but man as a whole being has a tendency to rhythm. For this reason it is good throughout life as a whole (and that is what we are concerned with when we educate and teach children) to attend to rhythmical repetition. That is why it is good to consider how quite specific educational motifs can be repeated year by year. Select things you want to take with the children, make a note of them and return to something similar every year. You can even adhere to this in the more abstract subjects. In a manner suited to the children's nature you teach addition in the first year. In the second year you come back to addition and teach more as well. And in the third year you return to it yet again. The same action is carried out repeatedly but in progressive repetitions.

To enter like this into the rhythm of life is of the greatest importance for all teaching and education, far more important than emphasising perpetually: Structure your lessons meaningfully so that you can immediately reveal whatever meaning is contained in all that you have to offer. We can only guess what this demand really means when we have gradually developed a feeling for life. And then by very reason of being teachers we shall avoid the external experimental approach that is so prevalent today, even in education. Once again I am pointing to these things not in order to condemn them but to improve certain aspects that have turned out to be detrimental to our spiritual culture. There are also educational textbooks on the results of memory experiments with 'experimental subjects'. These people are treated in a peculiar manner. Experiments are carried out with them to determine the manner in which they retain something of which they know the meaning. Then they are given a series of words that have no meaningful connection, and so on. Such experiments seeking to determine the laws of memory are practised very extensively today. Discoveries are made that are formulated as scientific theses. Just as for instance in physics we have Gay-Lussac's law and so on, attempts are now made to register similar laws in experimental psychology and education. In accordance with a certain quite justifiable scientific yearning, learned dissertations are expounded on the different forms of memory. First we have the memory type that assimilates with ease or with difficulty; secondly there is the type that finds it easy or difficult to reproduce what has been assimilated. So first of all 'experimental subjects' are tormented for the purpose of discovering that there are people who find it easy to memorize and others who find it difficult; then other 'subjects' are tormented in order to find out that there are those who find it either easy or difficult to recall what they have stored in their memory. And so through research we now know that there are memory types that assimilate with ease or with difficulty and that there are types that recall with ease or with difficulty what has been memorized. Thirdly there is the memory type that could be described as true and exact; fourthly there is the copious memory; and fifthly the memory that is retentive and reliable as opposed to the one that easily forgets. All this very much accords with the yearning of modern science to classify. We are now armed with scientific results and can state what has been found out scientifically in exact psychology about memory types: Firstly there is the type that assimilates with ease or with difficulty, secondly the one that recalls with ease or with difficulty, thirdly the type that is true and exact, fourthly the copious type, and fifthly the retentive type that may remember things for years as opposed to one that forgets easily.

Despite all due respect for this scientific method of investigation that devotedly and very conscientiously maltreats countless 'experimental subjects' and most ingeniously sets to work to obtain results so that we may know (now also in the field of education, since psychological experiments with children have shown that it applies to them too) what types of memory may be distinguished; despite all due respect for this scientific method I should nevertheless like to raise the following objection: Surely anyone endowed with a little sound common sense must know that certain people find it easy or difficult to memorize something or easy or difficult to recall something, others can repeat things truly and exactly in contrast to those who muddle everything up, yet others have a copious memory capable of retaining a long tale as opposed to those who can memorize only something short, and finally some remember things for a long time, perhaps years, while others forget everything within a week! This is old established knowledge as far as sound common sense is concerned. Yet it must be researched by scientific methods that inspire us all with respect, for it cannot be denied that they are very ingenious indeed.

Two comments are applicable here: Firstly it is better to cultivate sound common sense in education than to enter into experimentation of this kind which may very well develop ingenuity but does not bring us any nearer to the individual characteristics of the children. And then we may also say: Our era is in a sorry plight indeed if we have to assume that those who are to be teachers have so little sound common sense that they have to learn by such roundabout means of the existence of the different types of memory just described. These things certainly have to be regarded as symptoms of the state our spiritual culture is in.

I have been obliged to draw your attention to them, for you will find people saying to you: So you have found a position at the Waldorf School; it is the most amateurish institution,

they do not even want to hear about the greatest achieve-
ment of our time, namely experimental psychology. The
professional thing to do is to take up these methods, whereas
the way they teach at the Waldorf School is pure quackery!—
You will have to realize that it will sometimes be necessary
to recognize the relationship between science (that should
not be any the less respected) and what must be built up on
the basis of an inwardly oriented teaching and educational
practice. This creates an inner, loving attentiveness towards
the child as against the external relationships we learn about
through experimentation. Certainly the inward quality has
not entirely disappeared; indeed it is more prevalent than
we might think. But it is in definite opposition to the
scientific teaching that is being increasingly striven for. To a
certain extent it is true that the pursuit of scientific methods
at the present time can destroy a great deal, but it has not
the power to drive out every remnant of sound common
sense.

Let this be our starting point, for if we cultivate it well it
will lead us to an inner relationship with what ought to
happen in the lessons we teach. We must realize that we are
living at the beginning of a new age and that it is essential
for us to be thoroughly aware of this. Up to the middle of
the fifteenth century, surviving elements of Graeco-Roman
culture could still be felt. Since the middle of the fifteenth
century these have been no more than echos. But those who
even today live in these echos still have in certain lower
layers of their consciousness the tendency to hark back again
and again to that Graeco-Latin age which in its place was
wholly admirable but whose continuation today is no longer
something living. Think how self-satisfied people who have
learnt something are today if they can explain to you: If you
want to educate properly you must look not only at the
rhythm and the rhyme of a poem, you must also give a
suitable commentary as to the meaning and when you have

properly introduced your pupils to the meaning you will have reached the point at which they should actively take it into themselves; for even the ancient Romans (they will add after a long dissertation on the necessity of starting with an explanation of the meaning) used to say *rem tene, verba sequuntur*, once you have understood a thing, the words will follow of themselves. This is a tactic you will frequently encounter in people who consider themselves very learned and far above any dilettantism; first they expound on something as being the pinnacle of modern knowledge and then they add: Even the ancient Romans used to say. . . . Of course to be able to quote in Greek is even more a sign of supreme scholarliness. For the fourth post-Atlantean period this attitude was the right one, but it is not in keeping with our own time. The ancient Greeks did not send their children to the gymnasium to learn ancient Egyptian; they made them learn Greek. But we today first introduce our children to ancient languages. This is a fact that must be understood.

LECTURE SEVEN

Stuttgart, 28 August 1919

You will be faced with certain difficulties in your teaching that to start with your school by its very nature will have in common with rural schools. Urban schools nowadays do not have particularly good methods, while what might have been good in them is often spoilt by far-fetched ideas; but they do have the advantage of being well equipped with teaching aids, particularly for physics, chemistry and natural history. It is the same in primary schools as it is in secondary schools and scientific institutes: whereas the town schools have poorer methods and better equipment (though we should not ignore the goodwill of new teachers to find good methods), the country schools still, if their teachers have not been spoilt by training in a town before being posted to the country, sometimes have the better teaching methods even though they are less well equipped with teaching aids. Those who are seeking to come to grips with the problems and attitudes of our time have no laboratories and experimental equipment at their disposal, whereas those who are better equipped at universities and so on apply the least fruitful scientific methods. This state of affairs has existed for a long time in the scientific world and one cannot help wondering, for instance, what might not have grown out of Schopenhauer's[23] philosophy (which is now no more than a kind of philosophical dilettantism) if Schopenhauer had had all the means at his disposal that a professor of a few years' standing at a university nowadays has; and how little of a Schopenhauer spirit is brought forth

99

these days by university professors who have ample means at their disposal!

You will often have to rely on your powers of invention and fall back on simple devices in situations for which city schools have plenty of equipment. This may be just what you need to make your teaching really lively, but in some instances it will also thoroughly mar your pleasure in your work. You will feel this particularly when you have passed their ninth year with the children, when it is hardly possible to continue with the right kind of lessons without proper equipment. You will have to substitute drawings or simple, primitive paintings for all sorts of things when under ideal circumstances you would use the object itself in your lesson.

I have made this preliminary observation because today I want to speak to you about the transition in teaching method that must be observed particularly carefully when the children approach their ninth year. We shall not understand the curriculum here until we have schooled our educational capacities sufficiently to understand the being of the individual between his seventh and fifteenth years of life. I should like to show to you as teachers what you will have to apply in your lessons at the point when the children stand between their ninth and tenth years. Of course you will present it in a more elementary manner that they can understand. The point in question is reached by some children before their ninth year and by others later, but on average what I want to tell you about today starts with the ninth year.

When this period in the children's lives approaches we shall have to sense the necessity of introducing the subjects of natural history into our lessons. Before this period natural history is presented in a narrative form as I described yesterday in our seminar[24] when I spoke about the relationship of the animal and plant worlds to man. We use a narrative, descriptive form when we introduce natural history to the children earlier. But we cannot start giving proper lessons on natural history before they have crossed the Rubicon of their ninth year.

Now here it is enormously important to know that the aim to be accomplished in teaching the children about natural history will be thoroughly ruined if we do not start these natural history lessons by describing man himself. You may say quite rightly that there is not much you can tell a nine-year-old child about the natural history of man. But however little it may be, you must present it to him as a preparation for all your other natural history lessons. When you do this you must know that man represents a synthesis, a bringing-together of the three kingdoms of nature, that the three kingdoms of nature are brought together in man at a higher level. You will not have to tell this to the children but during the course of your lessons you will have to give them a feeling of how man is a synthesis of all the other kingdoms of nature. You will achieve this if you give the necessary emphasis to your description of man, if in the way you treat the subject of man you awaken in the children the impression of man's importance within the scheme of universal order. Perhaps you will start by describing man's external appearance to the nine-year-olds. You will draw their attention to the principal division of man into head, trunk and limbs, but in doing so you will always have to take account of the external appearance, the external form. You will do well to make use of the drawing activity you have already practised with the children to conjure up for them an idea of the main parts of the human form: that the head is round like a ball, that it is somewhat flattened on the underside where it rests on the trunk and is thus a ball perched on the trunk. It is good to give the children a mental picture like this. It awakens simultaneously the feeling and the will element, for they begin to see the head artistically from the point of view of its spherical shape. This is important. You appeal in this way to the child as a whole and not only to his intellect. Then you endeavour to awaken in the children the idea that the trunk is in a way a fragment of the head. You can do this by means of a drawing when you say: The head is round like a ball. If you take a piece out of the round ball (the shaded part of the drawing) by cutting it off and keeping what remains so that in a way the moon is left over from the sun, you have the essential form of the trunk.—It would be a good idea to make a round ball out of wax or kneaded dough and then cut off the shaded part so that you got the shape of the moon as it arises from the sphere; thus you could really call forth in the children the picture of the human trunk as a fragment of a

sphere. And for the limbs you have to awaken the idea that they are appended to the trunk and affixed to it. There will be a lot the children cannot understand, yet you will rouse the strong impression that the limbs are added on to the human organism. At this stage you should not go further regarding the fact that the limbs continue on inside the body as a morphological potentiality and are linked there with the sexual and digestive organs which are nothing other than an inward continuation of the limbs. But you must certainly rouse most strongly in the children the idea that the limbs are inserted into the organism from the outside. Thus you will have given the children a first conception of the human form.

Next you should awaken the idea, however elementary and primitive, that our faculty of looking at the world is bound up with that sphere that is our head. You can say to the children: Your eyes, your ears, your nose and your mouth are all in your head. You see with your eyes, you hear with your ears, you smell with your nose and you taste with your mouth. Most of what you know about the outside world you know through your head.—If you expand on this idea the children will gain a concept of the special formation and task of the head. Then you set about calling up in them an idea of the trunk by saying: What you taste with your tongue goes down into your trunk as food; what you hear with your ears goes into your trunk as sound.—It is good to create in the children the idea of the whole constellation of the organs in man. Thus it is good to indicate to them that in their chest they have organs for breathing and in their abdomen they have their stomach for digesting. Next you do well to let the children consider how man's limbs in the form of feet serve for walking and in the form of hands can move and work freely. It is good if the children can already come to an understanding of the difference between the way the feet serve the human being by carrying his body about and enabling him to go to the different places where he lives and works, and in contrast the service given by arms and hands with which man does not have to carry his body but with which he can instead work freely. While the feet are planted on the ground, the hands can be stretched out into the air so that they can work. In short, quite early on the children should be made aware of the essential difference between human legs and feet and human arms and hands. The difference between the service rendered by feet and legs when they carry man's body and that rendered by the hands and arms that do not work for man's body but for the world, this difference between the egoistic service of the feet and the selfless service of the hands that work for man's environment should be made clear to the children at an early stage through their feelings.

In this way, by letting the concept arise out of the form, we should teach the children as much as possible about the natural history of man. And only then do we pass on to the rest of natural history, specifically first to the animal kingdom. No doubt you will have to contrive some sort of make-shift, but it would be ideal if you could bring to the classroom a cuttle-fish, a mouse, lamb or horse or some other mammal, and some sort of image of man; but of course you will have plenty of human specimens, for all you need do is call out one of the children and present him to the others when you want man to be the object of their study. Now you must be quite clear about how you will proceed. First of all you will seek to familiarize the class with the cuttle-fish. You will tell them how it lives in the sea and show them what it looks like either by bringing a live one into the classroom or by making drawings. In short, you will introduce the cuttle-fish to the children. When you describe it to them they will feel that you are doing it in a particular way. They may not notice till much later, perhaps when you describe the mouse to them, how differently you treat the subject of the mouse from that of the cuttle-fish. You must endeavour to develop this artistic feeling in the children so that in the way you set about describing the cuttle-fish quite differently from the manner in which you describe the mouse you at the same time give them a certain feeling for the difference between these two animals. You must hint at the nature of the cuttle-fish by showing how it feels what surrounds it; if it scents danger it at once emits its dark juice, enveloping itself in a kind of aura to divert the attention of the approaching enemy. You can tell the children all sorts of things to help them understand that whatever the cuttle-fish does, perhaps protecting itself from its enemies in some way, or when it eats, it does it in the same way that the human being acts when he eats something or looks at something. When the human being eats he experiences a taste, a feeling that is communicated to him through his tongue, his organ of taste. And the human eye feels the constant need to look into the light; by doing this it comes to grips with light. Because man's organs of taste want to taste, they take in what serves as food. Well, you should describe the cuttle-fish in a way that gives the children a feeling for its sensitivity, its delicate perception of the things around it. You will have to work out an artistic description that will really enable the children to grasp the cuttle-fish.

Then you describe the mouse, giving a picture of its pointed snout and how clearly the whiskers on this pointed snout are to be seen and furthermore the gnawing teeth protruding from the lower and upper jaws. You describe its disproportionately large ears and then come to the cylindrical body with its fine velvety coat of hair. Next you describe its limbs, the smaller forefeet and the somewhat larger hindfeet that enable the mouse to jump well. It also has a scaly tail that is less hairy. You show the children how if the mouse wants to climb up something or grasp something with its forepaws it supports itself with this tail which is very useful because it is more sensitive inwardly owing to its being scaly and not hairy. In short, once again you seek to describe the mouse to the children by artistically building up its forms. You will succeed in this artistic construction if you awaken in the children a notion of how for all the functions for which the cuttle-fish does not need appendages attached to its body, the mouse does need such appendages. The cuttle-fish is sensitive in itself, through its body, so it does not need large ears like the mouse. Its relation to its environment allows it to imbibe nourishment without the help of a pointed snout. And it does not need such large, appended limbs as the mouse because it uses its body to propel itself along in the water. Sum up very thoroughly what you want to impart to the children in this artistic way, namely that the cuttle-fish manifests itself not through limbs but through the body itself.

I have to describe all this to you first so that you can translate it into teaching, for you must first be conscious of what you later have to bring more unconsciously into the lessons you prepare artistically. In a word, you must describe the mouse in a way that gradually awakens in the children the feeling: The mouse is organized in such a way that the limbs serve the life of the trunk.—Make it clear to the children that the lamb, too, is organized so that the limbs can serve the trunk, just as the horse when it lives in the wild also serves its trunk with its limbs. For instance you can show the children how the mouse has such very pointed teeth, teeth that have to be sharp and pointed, otherwise it would not be able to gnaw at objects as it must in order to nourish itself, or even bore holes to live in. With so much gnawing it keeps wearing down its teeth, but it is so arranged that like our nails its teeth keep growing again from within, so that the mouse constantly obtains an inner replacement for its tooth substance. This is particularly noticeable in the teeth, which are after all also organs that are appended to the rest of the organism and are formed in a way that enables the mouse's trunk to live.

In this way you have awakened in the children through their feelings a clear, though elementary, picture of the cuttle-fish and you have further awakened in them a clear picture of the structure of the mouse. Now you return once

again to the structure of man. You make clear to the
children: If we were to select the part of man that is most like
the cuttle-fish we would curiously enough find that this part
is the head of man. The part of man most like the cuttle-fish
is his head.—It is prejudice that causes people to imagine that
their head is the most perfect part of themselves. It is
certainly structured in a most complicated way, but it is
really just a metamorphosed cuttle-fish; I mean a metamorphosed lower animal. For the relation of the human head to
its environment is similar to that of the lower animals to
theirs. And with his trunk man is most like the higher
animals such as the mouse, the lamb, or the horse. But
whereas the cuttle-fish can entirely maintain its life through
its head, man cannot do this. His head must be set on top
of his trunk and rest there; it cannot move about freely. The
cuttle-fish, however, which is fundamentally an entire head
and nothing else, moves about freely in water. You will have
to make sure that the children gain a feeling for the fact that
the lower animals are heads moving about freely, though
they are as yet not as perfect as human heads. And you must
awaken in the children a feeling for the fact that the higher
animals are mainly trunks and have skilfully formed their
organs out of nature so that these may chiefly serve the
needs of the trunk, which is much less the case with the
human being; man is less perfect in his trunk than are the
higher animals.

Then we must arouse in the children a sense for what is in
fact the most perfect part of man's external form. Man is
most perfect in his limbs. If you follow the sequence of the
higher animals up to the apes you will find that the fore-
limbs are not so very different from the hind-limbs and that
the main function of all four is to carry the trunk, move
about with it and so on. This marvellous differentiation of
the limbs into feet and hands, legs and arms, only happens
in man; it expresses itself in his predisposition to walking

upright and having an upright posture. No animal species is so perfectly structured as man with regard to the complete organization of its limbs.

Here you should introduce a really vivid description of man's arms and hands: how they have no part in carrying the organism, how the hands do not touch the earth with regard to anything to do with the body, how they have been transformed in a way that enables them to grasp objects and undertake work. Then you move on to the moral element that has to do with the will. Awaken in the children through their feelings, not in theory, a strong picture: You can, for example, pick up a piece of chalk with your hand in order to write; you can only do this because your hand has been transformed to enable it to work instead of carrying the body about. An animal cannot be lazy as regards its arms because in fact it has not really got any. When we speak of an ape as a four-handed creature, this is only an inaccurate way of talking because it really has four armlike legs and feet and not four hands. For even if these creatures are structured for the purpose of climbing, this is really also only something that serves the body and their feet have been made handlike so that in climbing they can support the body. Man's hands and arms have become useless for whatever takes place in the human body and this is externally the most beautiful symbol of man's freedom! There is no more wonderful symbol of human freedom than man's arms and hands. Man can work for his environment with his hands and in that he nourishes himself, in that he eats, he can also work for himself out of his free will.

In this way, by describing the cuttle-fish, the mouse, lamb or horse, and the human being, we gradually awaken in the children a strong sense and feeling for the fact that the character of the lower animals is head-like, that of the higher animals is trunk-like, and that of man limb-like. It only inculcates conceit in people if they are constantly taught that man is the most perfect being on earth on account of his head. This causes people unwittingly to absorb the idea that man is perfect through laziness, through lethargy. For instinctively they know the head is a lazy-bones resting on the shoulders, not wanting to move about in the world but letting itself be carried by the limbs. It is not true that it is through his head, his lazy-bones of a head, that man is a perfect being; he is so through his limbs that are involved in the world and its work. You make a person inwardly more moral not by telling him that he is perfect through his lazy-bones of a head but that he is perfect through his active limbs. For those creatures that are only head and have to move themselves, like the lower animals, and the creatures that can only use their limbs in the service of their trunk, like the higher animals, are all less perfect compared with man because they can use their limbs less freely than he can. Their limbs have only a certain purpose, namely to serve the trunk. But with the human being one pair of limbs, his hands, is fully situated in the sphere of human freedom. You can only inculcate into human beings a healthy feeling for the world if you awaken in them the idea that they are perfect because of their limbs and not because of their heads. And you can do this very well through the comparative description of the cuttle-fish, the mouse, lamb or horse, and the human being. In doing this you will also notice that you should never exclude man when you describe something in any of the kingdoms of nature, for in man all the activities of nature are united. So we should always have man in the background when we describe anything in nature. This is also the reason why we must take man as our starting point when we start teaching the children about natural science after they have reached their ninth year.

If you observe the human being in his early years you will find that something takes place in him just between his ninth and tenth year. It is now not as obvious as it was when the first step of this process took place in earlier childhood. When the child starts to move his limbs somewhat more consciously, when he starts to walk, even if clumsily, when he starts to use his arms and hands purposefully, this is the point when he first becomes a little aware of his ego; to this point his memory will later reach back, and not beyond. When you see that the child normally starts to call himself 'I' at this age—though individuals vary—or a little later, since the will activity of speech first has to be developed, you will realize that the beginning of self-awareness at this point is clearly noticeable. On the other hand the change that takes place in the child's self-awareness now grows stronger and you will find that he understands much better what you mean when you speak to him about the difference between man and the world. Before he crosses the Rubicon of his ninth year, the child merges far more thoroughly with his environment than is the case later, when he begins to distinguish himself from his surroundings. Then you will find that you can begin to talk a little about things of the soul and he will not listen with such lack of understanding as he would before his ninth year. In short, the child's self-awareness grows deeper and stronger when he reaches his ninth year.

If you have a feeling for such things you will notice that at this age the children begin to use words in a much more inward way than before, becoming as they do more aware that words are something arising from within. Nowadays people are concerned far more about external than internal phenomena, and consequently they pay far too little heed to the change in the ninth or tenth year. But teachers must pay attention to it. And as a result they will be able to speak to the children with quite a different fundamental mood if they put off the teaching of natural history (that should always compare man with the other kingdoms of nature) until after this transition. Beforehand, while the children are still more merged with nature, we can only speak to them about the subjects of natural science in a narrative form; but after the ninth year we can present them with the cuttle-fish, the mouse, lamb or horse, and with the human being and it is permissible to speak of the relationship of the animals to the human form. Prior to this period you would come up against something incomprehensible to the children if you were to relate to the cuttle-fish whatever has to do with the head and to the mouse whatever has to do with the trunk, while also finding in man's limbs the element that raises him above the other kingdoms of nature. And you ought to make use of what this special age of the children offers you, because if you employ natural science lessons in the way I have described to you, you will then later implant into their souls moral concepts that are very firm and do not falter. You cannot instil moral concepts into the children by appealing to their intellect; you have to appeal to their feeling and their will. And you will appeal to the feeling and the will if you guide the children's thoughts and feelings to an understanding of how they themselves are only fully human when they use their hands for working in the world and how it is through this that man is the most perfect being, and also show them the relationship between the human head and the cuttle-fish, and between the human trunk and the mouse, sheep or horse. By feeling himself placed in the natural order of things in this way the child absorbs feelings that later help him to know himself as a human being.

You can instil this most particularly important moral element into the children's souls if you endeavour to shape the natural history lessons in a manner that will give them no clue that you want to teach them a moral lesson. But you will not be able to instil even a trace of anything moral into them if you teach natural history as something separate from man, if you describe the cuttle-fish by itself, the mouse, lamb or horse by itself and even man by himself; this would be nothing but an explanation of verbal definitions. For you can only explain man by building him up out of all the other organisms and functions in nature. *Schiller* admired in *Goethe* the way his conception of nature led him to build up man in a naive manner out of all the separate parts of nature; he expressed this admiration in the beautiful letter he wrote to Goethe at the beginning of the seventeen-nineties. I have mentioned this letter repeatedly because it contains something that ought to be totally absorbed into our culture: consciousness of the synthesis of all nature in man. Goethe again and again says that man stands at the summit of nature and there feels himself to be a whole world of nature. Or else he also says that the rest of the world reaches an awareness of itself in man. If you read what I have written you will find that over and over again I have included such quotations from Goethe. I did not quote them because I found them pleasing but because such ideas ought to be absorbed into the consciousness of our age. This is why it grieves me so much that one of the most important educational writings has remained virtually unknown or at least unfruitful in the educational field. Schiller learnt good educational principles from Goethe's naive self-education and he poured these educational principles into his *Letters on the Aesthetic Education of Man*. A tremendous amount that is fruitful for education is contained in these letters if only we can think beyond them and extend what they contain to its logical conclusions. Schiller arrived at his views through Goethe's vision. Just recall how Goethe, being as it were a portion of civilization implanted into nature, opposed the educational principles of his environment from earliest childhood. He could never bring himself to separate man from his environment. He always looked at man in his relationship to nature and he felt that he as a human being was one with nature. That is why he disliked his piano lessons so long as they were conducted as something quite apart from the nature of man. He only started to take an interest in these lessons when he was shown the functions of the different fingers, when he was told: This is Tommy Thumb, this is Peter Pointer—and so on and shown how Tommy Thumb and Peter Pointer were used for playing the piano. He always wanted the whole of man to be embedded in the whole of nature. You will remember the other thing that I have also mentioned: How when he was seven he built himself an altar to nature, taking his father's music stand and placing on it plants from his father's herbarium and also minerals and crowning it all with a little incense candle that he lit by focusing the beams of the morning sun with a burning-glass; an offering to the great god of nature, a rebellion against everything imposed on him by education. Goethe in the very way his nature manifested itself was always a human being longing to be educated in the way people ought to be educated nowadays. And it was because Goethe was like this, after he had broken himself in accordingly, that he appealed so much to Schiller who then wrote as he did about education in his aesthetic letters.

My old friend and teacher *Schröer*[25] once told me how as a teacher he had had to sit on a school commission to examine prospective teachers. He had however been prevented by circumstances from preparing what these future teachers were supposed to know in their examination. So instead he asked them questions about Schiller's aesthetic letters. They knew all about all sort of things, Plato and so on, but when Schröer started to question them about Schiller's aesthetic letters they rebelled! Soon the whole of Vienna knew: Schröer asked questions about Schiller's aesthetic letters in the teachers' examinations, but nobody can understand what they are about; no one can possibly understand such things!

But if what we are looking for are really healthy ideas on education, even if rudimentary, we cannot do without returning to such things as Schiller's aesthetic letters and also, for instance, Jean Paul's[26] educational doctrine *Levana*. The latter, too, contains an immense amount of practical educational suggestions. More recently, matters have improved to a certain extent, but it cannot be said that the kind of impulse that could come from Schiller's aesthetic letters and Jean Paul's educational teachings has passed over unadulterated into modern teaching practice.

I have today attempted to give you an idea of how you can 'read' from a certain period in a child's life, round about his ninth year, what it is best to do educationally in this period. Tomorrow we shall speak of how we can use the fourteenth and fifteenth years to teach the children what is then best suited to their being. In this way we shall approach an understanding of the way the whole period from seven to fifteen is structured and what we as teachers and educators should do. The curriculum is built on such considerations. Nowadays people often put the question in the abstract: How can we develop the child's capacities? But we must be quite clear that you first have to know what are the capacities of the growing individual before the abstract statement that these capacities must be developed can have any concrete meaning.

LECTURE EIGHT

Stuttgart, 29 August 1919

I have already pointed out that where schools fall under external legislation we must obviously agree to compromise both with regard to religious instruction and with regard to the curriculum. But we must keep clearly in mind what is right and best as a basis for the curriculum, so that where stipulations force us to do something inorganic we can perhaps discreetly correct the bad effects.

To find the right curriculum for the period of the seventh to the fourteenth or fifteenth year is a matter bound up in general with a true knowledge of child development over this period. Yesterday we threw some light on one moment in this development, the moment that falls between the ninth and the tenth year when the child has concluded his ninth year and is starting out on his tenth. If we follow the development of the child from the seventh year onwards through the eighth and ninth years, we come to the point before the tenth year is reached that I characterized for you as the one where ego-consciousness is strengthened and consolidated. From then on we can approach the child with concepts in natural science of the kind suggested yesterday with the cuttle-fish, the mouse, lamb or horse, and man himself. As you will have noticed, though, account must still be taken of the interplay between man and his environment and of how man is really a synthesis of all the other realms of nature and must therefore not yet be sharply detached from these other realms. A tremendous amount of harm is done to the growing being if we fail in his tenth and eleventh years to present him again and again through his feeling life with the way man is linked to external nature and is even a synthesis of this external world of nature.

But another important phase in the child's development lies between his twelfth and thirteenth years. During this period the spirit and soul elements in man are reinforced and strengthened, that is to say those spirit and soul elements that are less dependent on the ego. What in spiritual science we are accustomed to calling the astral body permeates the etheric body and unites with it. Of course the astral body as an independent being is not born until puberty, but it manifests itself in a peculiar manner through the etheric body by permeating and invigorating it between the twelfth and thirteenth years. Here, then, lies another important milestone in the child's development. It expresses itself in the way the child, if we treat rightly what is now in him, begins to develop an understanding for the impulses working in the external world that resemble impulses of spirit and soul such as those at work in the external world as the forces of history. I have given you an example[27] of how the working of these historical forces can be brought within the scope of teaching at elementary school level. But although you will have to transpose what I said to you into childlike language, you can be as childlike as you will in your expressions and you will achieve nothing in the way of awakening in the children a proper understanding of historical impulses if you approach them with historical observations before they have completed their twelfth year. Prior to this you can tell them about history in the form of stories, biographies for instance. This they would be able to grasp. But they will be unable to grasp historical connections before they complete their twelfth year. Therefore you will do damage if you fail to observe this turning point. The children now begin to develop a yearning to have explained to them as history what they have earlier taken in as stories.

So if you have told the children stories, for instance about one or other of the crusaders or other historical figures, you must now endeavour to transform this material in a way that will allow them to perceive the historical impulses and historical links involved. When you observe such a phenomenon and notice unmistakably that if you do things properly the children understand you from their twelfth year onwards, you will say to yourselves: Up to the children's ninth year I shall in the main restrict myself to what we have discussed as the artistic element and out of this bring writing and reading and later also arithmetic; I shall not make the transition to natural history until after the point is reached that we discussed yesterday; and I shall wait with history, except in the form of stories, until they have reached their twelfth year.—At this point the children begin to take an inner interest in great historical connections. This will be quite specially important for the future for it will become more and more obviously necessary to educate people in an understanding of historical coherence, for hitherto they have never really achieved a proper conception of history. So far they have first and foremost been members of economic life and national life in which they have participated mechanically, coping quite adequately with the requirements and interests of this economic and national life by knowing a few anecdotes about rulers and wars—which is not history—and a few dates of kings and one or two famous people and battles.

Lessons in future will have to be particularly concerned with the way in which the cultural life of mankind has developed. They will have to include proper teaching on the impulses of history and these impulses will have to find their proper place in the curriculum so that they are given at the right moment.

Something else now also begins to be comprehensible to the child when he has crossed this Rubicon of reaching his twelfth year. However clearly you explain the functioning of the human eye to the child before this point, he will be unable to understand it properly. For what does it mean to teach the child about the functioning of the human eye? It means showing him how beams of light fall into the eye and are taken up and refracted by the lens, how they then pass through the vitreous body and work as a picture on the rear wall and so on. You have to describe all these processes in terms of physics. You are describing a process in physics that takes place in man, in one of man's sense organs. If you want to describe this process then you must first teach the child the concepts that will enable him to take in this kind of description of the eye. This means that you must first teach him what the refraction of light beams is. It is quite simple to do so by showing him a lens, explaining the focus and demonstrating how light is refracted. But these are facts of physics that have their place outside man. We can describe them to the child between the point after his ninth year and that before his twelfth. But we should not apply such descriptions of physics to the organs of the human being before the child has completed his twelfth year because only then does he begin to assess in the right way how the external world is continued in man. Before his twelfth year he cannot understand this. He can understand the processes of physics but he cannot understand how these processes take place within man.

The comprehension of the historical impulses of mankind and the comprehension of nature's laws of physics working in the human organism are akin to one another. The real essence of humanity lives in historical impulses; what is gathered together in these impulses lives in external historical events that in turn have their effect on individual human beings. And when you describe the human eye you describe an activity of external nature that is also working

within man. Both processes require similar powers of comprehension, and these powers only start to develop in the
child's twelfth year. So it will be necessary to arrange the
curriculum in a way that will include for the period
between the ninth and twelfth years lessons on the simple
concepts of physics necessary for an understanding of man
himself; thus in addition to natural history, simple physics
will be taught, but the application of the laws of physics to
man will wait till after the twelfth year. In the same way
stories will be told up to the twelfth year in order then to be
transformed into history.

My explanations so far refer to the way subjects are
introduced. Of course we can then continue to enlarge on
physics after the twelfth year. But neither physics nor
natural history should be started before the ninth year, and
neither history nor lessons involving physiology, that is
descriptions of human functions, should start before the
twelfth year is completed. If you take into account that
comprehension is something that blossoms not only in man's
intellect but always also includes feelings and will, you will
find that you are not too remote from what I have just said.
When people do not take such things into account it is
because they have succumbed to illusions. You can in a
makeshift way present the human intellect with historical or
physiological facts before the twelfth year, but by doing so
you spoil human nature, strictly speaking you make it
unsuitable for the whole of life. But between the ninth and
twelfth year you can gradually introduce for instance the
concepts of refraction, and the formation of images through
lenses or other instruments. You could perhaps discuss the
way an opera glass works with the nine to twelve-year-olds.
And you can also talk with them about the way a clock
works and explore the difference between a pendulum clock
and a pocket watch, and anything like this. But before they
reach their twelfth year you should not describe to them

how refraction and image formation can also be applied to the human eye.

All this will have provided you with points of reference from which you can learn how the material to be taught should be distributed in the curriculum so that the capacities of the children are developed in the right way. And there is more to be observed from this point of view. It is to a certain extent important that we should not move too far away from life in our lessons, though on the other hand we should not take excessive account of the trivialities of life either. To say to a child: What have you got on your feet?—and expect him to answer: A pair of boots,—What are the boots for?—For me to put on,—is called by some teachers an object lesson and is in reality nothing but a triviality. The kind of object lessons sometimes described in educational books bore the children frightfully in their subconscious and as a result a great deal in them is damaged. Remaining too close to life in this way and constantly bringing things to consciousness that could quite well remain in the unconscious, bringing activities that are merely habitual too much into consciousness, is something we should not let ourselves in for. On the other hand we need not lose all contact with life and teach the children empty abstractions too early on. This will be especially important with regard to physics lessons. Indeed, physics lessons will anyway supply opportunities for combining very closely things that are near to life with things that are in the first instance rather removed from external life. You should therefore take care to develop the concepts of physics from life itself. You should do as much as your inventiveness will allow to let the children experience things, for instance how after we have lit the stove in our classroom the floor remains cold even when the air near the ceiling is quite warm. You thus draw their attention to a fact of life and starting from this fact of life you can then continue to explain that of

course the air round the stove gets warm first and not the air
near the ceiling but that warm air always strives upwards
and thus makes the cold air fall down. So you must describe
the process as follows: The air first gets warm down below
round the stove, then it rises to the ceiling making the cold
air fall down, and that is why a room is still cold near the
floor even when the air near the ceiling has been warm for
some time. In this way you have started from a fact of life
and from there you now seek the transition to the fact that
warm air expands and cold air contracts. This statement
takes you rather further away from life. Another example is
when you discuss the lever in physics. It is not good just to
present the abstract lever. Start with a pair of scales and
move on from there to the lever. Start with something that
is used in everyday life and proceed from there to whatever
can be thought out from it in physics.

Now I must not omit to point out to you that a consider-
able amount of what is included in our concepts of physics
wreaks havoc in the child and that a great deal depends on
the teacher himself knowing what is right and endeavouring
to be mature in his judgments. You cannot avoid saying to
the bigger children: Here you have an electricity machine;
what I have here is a frictional electricity machine. I can
make electricity by rubbing certain objects but I must first
wipe the objects carefully because they have to be quite dry.
If they are wet the experiment will not work and no
electricity will be made.—Then you enlarge on the reasons
why electricity cannot be produced with wet instruments.
And now you go on to explain how lightning occurs,
pointing out that it is also an electrical process. Now many
people maintain that the clouds rub against one another
and that this friction brings about lightning as an electrical
discharge. The child will perhaps believe this because the
teacher himself believes it. But in his subconscious something special takes place of which he is of course unaware.

He says to himself: Well, my teacher wipes his instruments before rubbing them to make electricity to make sure that they are not wet, and then he tells me that if clouds rub together, electricity is made. But clouds are wet!—The child notices such inconsistencies. And much of the disunity in life stems from the fact that children are told such contradictions. These contradictions ought to arise outside in the world; in our thinking they have no place! But because man's knowledge and recognition is today too shallow, such contradictions, that really rend the unconscious inner being of man, continually crop up in what we tell the children and later the young people. Therefore we must at least take care that what we bring consciously to the children does not contain too much of what in their subconscious they will imagine differently. It will not be our task as teachers to eliminate from science such things as the nonsense that is maintained concerning the link between lightning and electricity in physics. But when we deal with more obvious things we should always remind ourselves that we influence not only the children's conscious but always also their subconscious being. How can we take account of this subconscious?

We can only do so as teachers by becoming more and more the kind of people who do not adjust things in order to make them understandable for the child. I have already mentioned in another connection what this involves. You must develop in yourselves capacities that allow you, the moment you enter upon a subject with the children, to become as absorbed by the subject as the child is by the lesson, regardless of what the subject is that you are treating. You should not allow yourself to be filled with the thought: Of course I know a great deal more but I am arranging it to suit the children; I make myself quite superior to the children and prepare everything I want to say to them so that it will be suitable for them.—No! You must have the ability to transform yourself in such a way that the children literally wake up through your lesson and that you yourself become a child with the children, but not in a childish way. Governesses often err in this respect, talking baby language with their charges. If the child says 'dada' they also say 'dada' instead of 'father'. It is not a matter of becoming childish with the children in an external way; we must transform what is more mature into something childlike. To be capable of doing this in the right way we have to look rather more deeply into the nature of man. We have to take seriously the fact that just with regard to his most important spiritual characteristic man becomes productive by retaining the childlike element all his life. We are a poet, an artist if we can always relive in ourselves the activity of the child with our maturer humanity. To be for ever a steady fellow, unable any longer to use in a childlike, an inner childlike way our thinking, feeling and willing (that has absorbed maturer concepts now that we are over thirty), to be for ever a steady fellow is not a suitable mood of life for a teacher. The proper mood of life for him is always to be able to return to childhood with everything he experiences and with everything he learns. He will of course not return to childhood when he is by himself by describing in baby language something new he has learnt; he will return because with every new fact he will experience as much delight and intense joy as the child does when he perceives a new fact of life. In a word, it is the soul and spirit that should return to childhood and not the external physical manifestation.

Then, too, a great deal will depend on the atmosphere that is created between teacher and pupils. It is right, for instance, if you speak about life and about nature in such a way that you take as much pleasure in it as the children themselves and are as much amazed as the children themselves. Let me give you an example: You have all learnt

some physics and thus know a fair amount about what is
called morse telegraphy. You know what happens when a
telegram is sent from one place to another, how the telegram operator uses the different devices, pressing the morse
key now for a short time, now for longer, thus closing the
circuit for shorter or longer moments, whereas the circuit is
interrupted when he does not press the key. You know that
the actual morse telegraph apparatus is linked to the circuit
by an iron lever attracted by a coil that contains an
electro-magnet and that the so-called relay is connected into
this current. You know that with the help of a wire one such
apparatus at one station is linked with another at another
station so that what is produced at the first station is
reproduced at the second. By connecting the current for
shorter or longer moments I cause something to be received
at the next station which when it is transposed can be read
by the operator there. The shorter or longer bursts of
current become visible as impressions on a strip of paper as
dots or dashes. The strip of paper runs through rollers. You
see, for instance, a dot and then after an interruption three
dots, and so on. The alphabet consists of dots and dashes;
thus an *a* is ·—, *b* is —·· , *t* is just a dash and so on. Thus
you can read what is transmitted from one station to the
next.

Yet everything that is said about this telegraphy apparatus is really only a question of intellectual consideration.
You certainly do not require many soul forces in order to
make comprehensible all the mechanical things that take
place in it when the mechanism is permeated by electricity,
which itself can so far only be explained hypothetically by
science. But one thing does remain a miracle; such things
really can be described as miracles. And I must say, when I
think of the link that is created between the morse apparatus at one station and that at another station, it never fails
to fill me with wonder when I realize how the circuit is

closed. For the electrical circuit is not closed by means of a wire running from one station to the next and another running back again. This would also be possible and the interruption could then be brought about by breaking the closed circuit. But this closed circuit containing the morse apparatus is not brought about by wires that run back and forth; only one part of the current runs along a wire. At each station the wire ends in a metal plate in the earth, so that the link which could be made through a wire is provided by the earth itself. What would otherwise be brought about by the other half of the wire is done by the earth itself. Whenever you think of how a morse apparatus at one station is linked to another at another station you are reminded of the miracle that makes the earth, the whole earth into a mediator, taking the electric current as though into its care and duly delivering it at the next station. The earth itself mediates in this way. All the explanations that exist for this are hypothetical. But the important thing as regards our human attitude towards it is that we should be able ever and again to feel how miraculous this fact is, that we should not become blunted in our ability to grasp the processes of physics with our feelings. Then when we explain these things to the children we shall find the mood that again and again allows us to return to the way we first took in a fact when we grasped it. Then when we explain a phenomenon of physics to a child who is full of wonder we shall ourselves become children full of wonder. Such marvels are hidden in all things including the processes of physics that take place in the world.

Imagine for a moment that you are giving the following lesson. Over there is a bench or something like that, and on the bench lies a ball. I pull the bench away sharply, and the ball falls to the ground. What would most teachers say today to explain this to a child? They would say: The ball is attracted to the earth; if it is not lying on something it is subject to the force of gravity. But that does not really explain anything. For this sentence stating that the ball is subject to the force of gravity has actually no meaning. It is one of those verbal definitions we have already spoken about. For, once again, the physicists say of gravity and its nature that nothing is known about it; and yet they talk about it. However, we cannot avoid speaking of gravity; we must mention it. Otherwise when our pupils go out into life they may be asked, at some point when they are being assessed for some post, to explain what gravity is. Just imagine what would happen if a fifteen-year-old youngster did not know what gravity was! There would be the devil of a fuss. So we must explain gravity to the children; we must not be foolish enough to close our eyes to the demands of the world as it is today. But by working on their subconscious we can awaken beautiful concepts in the children. Owing to the fact that we have already taught them other things, we can make the following clear to them: Here you have the receiver of an air pump with no air in it. If you take out the stopper, air flows in rapidly, filling up what was empty. This is related to what happens also in the other case when we speak of the working of gravity; if we pull away the bench, something also streams in. The difference is only that in the one case the air outside flows into an empty space whereas in the other case the effect only works in one direction.—Now you compare the two phenomena.[28] Do not give the children verbal definitions but show them the connections between the concepts and the phenomena that have to do with the air and the phenomena that take place with the solid bodies. Once we have grasped the concept of solid bodies streaming in the direction in which they strive to go if they are not prevented from doing so, then we could dispense with the concept of air streaming into an empty space and healthier concepts would arise than are today poured into the world, such as for instance Professor

Einstein's complicated Theory of Relativity. I mention this as a passing comment on the present state of our civilization for I cannot avoid pointing out how many harmful things live in our culture (such as for instance the Theory of Relativity, particularly in its most recent version) and how these things run their ruinous course if the child has become a research scientist.

You have now been introduced to a large part of the basis and method for working out the curriculum.

LECTURE NINE

Stuttgart, 30 August 1919

The children coming to the Waldorf School will be of widely different ages. When we start the lessons in the different classes we shall have to take particular account of this age range, and we must also not lose sight of something else in this connection.

Unfortunately we cannot straight away found a university with all the usual faculties to follow on from the Waldorf School. So it will be up to us to prepare our pupils for other institutes of further education that they will have to attend when they leave the Waldorf School and before they step out into life. Thus we must bring our pupils to the point when they leave of having the necessary qualifications for whatever further education institution will be suitable for them when they go out into life. We shall nevertheless achieve our aim and accomplish our task, despite the need to conform to these restrictions, if we can put into practice something of the educational principles we have founded on the present cultural epoch of mankind's development. We shall only be able to achieve this, though, particularly as regards the older children who come to us and who will soon have to be sent out into the other institutions of life, if we apply a golden rule: to teach economically.

We shall be able to teach economically if particularly with the thirteen, fourteen and fifteen-year-olds we carefully eliminate everything that is merely ballast for human soul development at that age and can bear no fruits for life. For instance we shall have to make room in our time-table at least for Latin, and possibly also for Greek. We must in any case really come to grips with language teaching, for this will be a most significant feature of our method as a whole. Let us look at the fact that you will be having pupils who will already have been taught French or Latin up to a certain stage. Their lessons will have been conducted in a certain way. You will now have to spend your first lesson or even your first week finding out what they can already do. You will have to repeat with them what they have done so far. But you must do this economically so that each according to his capacity will benefit even from this repetition.

Now you will achieve a great deal simply by taking into account that what delays you more than anything else in foreign-language teaching is translation from the foreign language into the mother tongue and vice versa. An enormous amount of time is wasted when, for instance, so much translation from Latin into German and from German back into Latin is expected of grammar school pupils. Instead there should be much more reading and the pupils should spend much more time expressing their own thoughts in the foreign language. How then will you set about teaching a foreign language, let us say French, on the basis of this rule?

Let us first consider the older children to whom this will apply, the thirteen and fourteen-year-olds. For them you will first of all have to select carefully what you want to read with them in the language in question. You select passages for reading and then call up the pupils in turn to read them aloud. You will now save the pupils' time and energy if you do not at first insist on a translation into German of the passages in question but instead see to it that each child reads properly with regard to pronunciation and so on. Next with the classes in which you want to let revision intermingle with new ground to be covered it would be good if you still did not turn to translation but instead let the pupils give a free rendering of the content in the passage they have read.

Just let the children repeat in their own words what the passage contains while you listen carefully in case anything is omitted that might indicate that something has not been understood. It is more convenient for you, of course, simply to let the children translate, for then you soon see where one of them cannot go on. It is less convenient to watch in case something is being omitted instead of just waiting till the child comes to a stop, but you can nevertheless find out by this means whether something has not been understood if a phrase is not rendered in the mother tongue. There will of course be children who make a very capable rendering of the passage; this does not matter. And there will be others whose rendering is much freer in the use of their own words; this, too, does not matter. This is the way we should discuss the text with the children.

Next we tackle the opposite procedure. First we discuss some subject with the children in their mother tongue, some subject that they can follow through with us in their thoughts and feelings. Then we can try to let the children repeat freely (depending how far advanced they already are) in the foreign language what we have been discussing with them. In this way we shall discover how well these children, who have come to us from all sorts of classes, know the foreign language.

Now you cannot teach a foreign language in school without really working at grammar, both ordinary grammar and also syntax. It is particularly necessary for children of over twelve to be made conscious of what lies in grammar. But here too you can proceed very economically. Now although this morning in our study of man[29] I said that in ordinary life we form conclusions and then proceed to judgment and concept, you can of course not give the children this logical teaching, but it will underlie your teaching of grammar. You will do well to discuss matters of the world with the children in a way that, particularly with

the help of the lessons in foreign languages, will enable
grammar lessons to arise as a matter of course. It is purely a
matter of structuring such a thing in the right way. Start by
shaping with the children something that is a complete
sentence and not more than a sentence. Point to what is
going on outside—at this very moment you would have an
excellent example! You could very well combine grammar
with a foreign language by letting the children express in
Latin and French and German for example: It is raining.
Start by eliciting from the children the statement: It is
raining, it rains. And then point out to them (they are after
all older children) that they are expressing a pure activity
when they say: It rains. And now (including if you like the
foreign languages, for you will save a great deal of time and
energy if you also work this into the foreign language lesson)
proceed to another sentence that you can arrive at if you
say: Now instead of the scene outside in the rain, imagine to
yourselves a meadow in springtime.—Lead the children until
they say of that meadow: It is greening, it greens.—And then
lead them further until they transform the sentence: It
greens—into the sentence: The meadow greens. And finally
lead them still further till they can transform the sentence:
The meadow greens—into the idea or concept: The green
meadow.

   If you stimulate these thoughts I have just introduced to
you one after the other in your language lessons, you will
not be pedantically teaching the children syntax and logic;
you will be guiding the whole soul constellation of the
children in a direction that will mean you are teaching them
in an economical way what they should have in their soul.
You introduce 'It . . .' or 'It is . . .' sentences to the children,
sentences that really live only in the domain of activity and
are sentences in themselves without any subject or predicate,
sentences that belong to the living realm of conclusions and
are indeed abbreviated conclusions. With an example where

this is possible you make the further step of finding a
subject: The meadow greens, the meadow that is green.—
With this you have taken the step of forming a judgment
sentence. You will agree that it would be difficult to con-
struct a similar judgment sentence for: It rains. For where
would you find the subject for: It rains? It is not possible.
Thus by practising in this way with the children we enter
linguistic realms about which philosophers have written a
great deal. *Miklosič*, the scholar of Slav languages,[30] for
instance, started writing about subjectless sentences. Then
Franz *Brentano*[31] took up the subject, and then particularly
Marty[32] in Prague. They all sought to find the rules connected with subjectless sentences such as: It rains, it snows,
it lightens, it thunders and so on—for out of their logic they
could not understand where subjectless sentences came
from.

Subjectless sentences, as a matter of fact, arise from the
very intimate links we have with the world in some respects,
man being a microcosm embedded in a macrocosm so that
his activity is not separated from the activity of the world.
When it rains, for instance, we are very closely linked with
the world, particularly if we have no umbrella; we cannot
separate ourselves from it and get just as wet as the pave-
ments and houses around us. Thus in such a case we do not
separate ourselves from the world, we do not invent a
subject but name only the activity. Where we can be
somewhat more separate from the world, where we can
more easily escape from it, as in the case of the meadow,
there we can invent a subject for our sentence: The meadow
greens.

From this you see that in the way we speak to the
children we can always take account of the interplay
between man and his environment. So by presenting the
children (particularly in the lessons devoted to foreign languages) with such examples in which grammar is linked

with the practical logic of life, we, endeavour to discover how much they know of grammar and syntax. But in the foreign language lessons please avoid first working through a reading passage and subsequently pulling the language to pieces. Make every effort to develop the grammatical side independently. There was a time when foreign language textbooks contained fantastic sentences that took account only of the proper application of grammatical rules. Gradually this came to be regarded as ridiculous and sentences taken more from life were included in the foreign language textbooks instead. But here too the middle path is better than the two extremes. Thus if you use only sentences from ordinary life you will not be able to teach pronunciation very well unless you also use sentences like the ones we spoke yesterday as an exercise;[33] for instance

Lalle Lieder lieblich,
Lipplicher Laffe,
Lappiger, lumpiger,
Laichiger Lurch

that takes account solely of the essence of language. When you carry on grammar and syntax with the children you will, then, have to make up sentences specifically to illustrate this or that grammatical rule. But you will have to see to it that the children do not write down these sentences illustrating grammatical rules. Instead of being put down in their copy books they should be worked on; they come into being but they are not preserved. This procedure contributes enormously to the economical use of your lessons, particularly those for foreign languages, for in this way the children absorb the rules in their feelings and after a while drop the examples. If they are allowed to write down the examples, they absorb the form of the example too strongly, whereas for the teaching of grammar the examples ought to be dispensable; they should not be carefully written down in copy books, for only the rule should finally remain. So it is good for the living language, actual speaking, to use exercises and reading passages as just described, and on the other hand to let the children formulate their own thoughts in the foreign language, using more the kind of subject that crops up in daily life. For grammar, however, you use sentences that from the start you intend the children to forget and therefore you do not let them do what is always a help in memorizing: write them down. For all the activity involved in teaching the children grammar and syntax with the help of sentences takes place in living conclusions; it should not descend into the dreamlike state of habitual actions but continue to play in fully conscious life.

Naturally this does introduce into the lessons something that makes teaching somewhat strenuous. But you cannot avoid the fact that particularly in the lessons with the pupils who come into the older classes there will be a certain amount of effort needed. You will have to proceed very economically. Yet this economy will actually benefit only the pupils. You yourselves will need a great deal of time in order to invent all the things that will help make the lessons as economical as possible. Therefore on the whole let grammar and syntax lessons be conversational. It will thus not be a good thing to give the children actual grammar and syntax books in the form in which they exist today; they also contain examples, but examples are something that should on the whole be discussed and not written. Only the rules should be written down in the copy book the children use for regular grammar and syntax learning. Thus it will be exceedingly economical and you will also do the children an enormous amount of good if today you discuss a particular rule of grammar in a language with the help of an example you have invented, and if then tomorrow or the next day in the same language lesson you return to this rule and let the child use his own 'upper storey' to find an example. Do not on any account underestimate the educa-

tional value of such a method. Teaching is very much
indeed a matter of subtleties. It is vastly different whether
you merely question the child on a rule of grammar and let
him repeat from his copy book the examples you have
dictated to him, or whether you make up examples specially
intended to be forgotten and now get the child to find his
own examples. The activity is something immensely educational. You will soon see: Even if you have in your class the
worst young scamps who never pay any attention at all,
when you set them the task of finding examples to fit a rule
of syntax (and you can do this very well if you yourself are
fully alert as you teach) they will start to take pleasure in
these examples and especially in the activity of making them
up themselves. When the children now come to school after
the long summer holidays, having played and romped out of
doors for weeks on end, you will have to realize that they
have little inclination after these weeks of playing and
romping to sit quietly in class and listen attentively to things
that they are expected to remember. But even if you find
this rather disturbing during the first week and perhaps also
in the second week, if you conduct particularly your foreign
language lessons in a way that lets the children share in the
soul activity by making up examples, you will discover
among them after three or four weeks a number who enjoy
making up such examples just as much as they enjoyed
playing and romping out of doors. But you too must take
care to make up some examples as well and not hesitate to
make the children aware of this. It is very good for the
children once they have got into the swing of this activity if
they want to go on and on so that it might happen that
while one is giving an example another already calls out: I
have one too.—And now they all want a turn to say their
examples. It is then good if you say at the end of the lesson:
I am ever so pleased that you like doing this just as much as
you enjoyed romping out of doors!—A remark like this echoes

on in the children; they carry it with them all the way home
from school and tell it to their parents at lunch. You really
must say things to the children that they like to tell their
parents at the next meal. And if you actually succeed in
interesting them so much that they ask their mother or
father at the next meal: Can you make up an example for this
rule?—then you really have carried off the prize. You can
achieve such successes if you throw yourself heart and soul
into your teaching.

Only consider what a difference it makes if you discuss
with the children in a spirited way the process of: It rains, it
greens, the meadow is greening, the green meadow—instead
of developing grammar and syntax in the usual way by
pointing out: this is an adjective, this is a verb, if a verb
stands alone there is no sentence—in short if, instead of
piecing things together as is often done in grammars, you
develop the theme in a lively lesson. Compare this living
way of teaching grammar with the way it is so often taught
nowadays: The Latin or French teacher comes into the
classroom; the children have to get out their Latin or
French books; they have done their homework and now
they are to translate, and then they have to read. Soon all
their bones ache because the seats are so hard. If proper
education and teaching had been going on, there would
have been no need to take such care in designing chairs and
desks. The fact that so much care has had to be lavished on
the making of seats and desks is proof that education and
teaching have not been done sensibly, for if children are
really taken up in their lessons the class is so lively that even
if they are sitting down they do not sit firmly. We should be
delighted if our children do not sit down firmly, for only
those who are themselves sluggish want a class of children to
remain firmly seated, after which they drag themselves
home aching in every limb. Particular account must be
taken of these things in grammar and syntax lessons. Now

imagine that the children have to translate; grammar and syntax are worked out from the very things they ought to be enjoying! After this they are most unlikely to go home and say to their fathers: We're reading such a lovely book; let's do some translating together.—It really is to the point not to lose sight of the principle of economy and this will serve you particularly well in your teaching of foreign languages.

We must of course see to it that our teaching of grammar and syntax is fairly complete. Therefore we shall have to find out what gaps the pupils have who are now going to come to us from all sorts of other classes. Our first task will be to close the gaps, particularly in grammar and syntax; so that after a few weeks we shall have brought a class to a stage where there are no old gaps and we can thus proceed. But if we teach in the way I have described (and we are quite capable of this if we are totally involved in the lessons and if we ourselves are interested in them) then we shall be giving the children in the right way what they will need to enable them to pass the usual college entrance examinations later on. And we give the children a great deal else besides that they would not receive in ordinary elementary or secondary schools, things that make them strong for life and give them something that will serve them throughout life. It would be particularly good with regard to foreign languages if the lessons could be organized in a way that would allow the different languages the children have to learn for one reason or another to stand side by side. An enormous amount of time is lost if thirteen, fourteen, fifteen-year-old boys and girls have to be taught Latin by one teacher, French by another and English by a third. Much, very much would be gained if one and the same thought developed by a teacher with a pupil in one language could be developed by another pupil in another language and a third in a third language. One language would thus abundantly support the other. Of course such things can only be done if one has the necessary means, in this case the teachers. But whatever is available should be fully utilized. The support that one language can give another should be taken into account. By this means it is possible in grammar and syntax lessons to point constantly from one language to another, and this touches on something that is exceedingly important for the pupil.

He learns a thing far better if he has in his soul the method of applying it in a number of directions. Thus you will be able to say to him: Now you have spoken a German sentence and a Latin sentence. In a German sentence if we are speaking of ourselves we can hardly ever leave out the 'I', but in the Latin sentence this 'I' is contained in the verb.—You need not go any further. Indeed it would not be good to go any further. But it is good just to touch on this fact so that the pupil gains a certain feeling for it; then something will emanate from this feeling that will work as a living faculty for understanding other elements of grammar. And I beg you to absorb this fact and think it over very deeply: that it is possible in a stimulating, living lesson to develop during its course the capacities you need for teaching. This is indeed so. If, for example, you have touched upon something without pedantically enlarging on it when you have said to the children: Latin does not say 'I' because it is included in the verb, but the German language does say it, then for a moment a faculty is awakened in the children that is otherwise not there. At this moment the faculty is awakened, and afterwards when something like this has awakened, you can work at grammatical rules more easily with the children than if you had to draw on their ordinary state of soul. You will have to think how you can create the aptitudes you want for a certain lesson. The children need not have the full measure of capacities you intend to use; but you must have the skill to call to life such capacities that can later fade away again when the children leave the classroom.

This can be applied particularly to the teaching of foreign languages when you let this include: reading aloud by the children (with attention paid to proper pronunciation whereby rather than giving too many pronunciation rules you read a section and then let the children read after you), retelling of the passage read, and letting the children form their own thoughts about it and then express them in different languages; and quite separate from this the lessons on grammar and syntax with rules to be remembered and examples to be forgotten. So much for the framework of our language teaching.

LECTURE TEN

Stuttgart, 1 September 1919

Let us try to proceed with our treatment of teaching methods by from now on keeping one eye more on the curriculum and the other more on what will be the actual teaching material within it. The curriculum will not at first contain everything, for we shall build up the way we view things by degrees.

I started by giving you considerations that enabled us to find something belonging to the different stages of teaching. How many such stages can be distinguished from the beginning of schooling up to the age of fourteen, fifteen? From what we have meanwhile come to realize we see that an important turning point occurs round about the ninth year; we can thus say: The first stage of schooling lasts up to the ninth year. What do we do during that period? Our starting point will be the artistic realm. We shall work musically and in painting and drawing with the children in the way we have discussed. We shall allow writing to arise gradually out of painting and drawing. Step by step the forms of writing will arise out of the forms of our drawings, and then we shall move on to reading.

It is important for you to understand the reasons for this sequence so that you do not start with reading and then link it with writing but rather proceed from writing to reading. Writing is in a sense still something more living than reading. Reading isolates the human being very much and draws him away from the world. In writing we have not yet ceased to imitate universal forms if we let it arise out of drawing. But printed letters have indeed become extraordinarily abstract. They have, though, arisen out of written letters and so we too let them arise out of the written letters in our lessons. It is entirely right if at least for writing lessons you keep the thread intact that leads from the drawn shape to the written letter, so that the children in a way still sense the original drawn form in the letters. In this way you overcome what is so alien to the world in writing. In the process of finding their way into writing, the children assimilate something that is very alien to the world. But if we link the written shapes to the universal forms such as F = fish and so on, we are at least leading them back towards the world. And it is so very important that we do not sever the children's links with the world. The further we go back into civilization, the more living are the links we find binding man to the world. You need only call before your souls one particular picture in order to understand what I mean by this. Instead of seeing me here talking to you, imagine yourselves back in ancient Greece where a rhapsodist is declaiming Homer to his audience in that strange manner we no longer have, part song, part speech; and imagine sitting by the side of this rhapsodist declaiming Homer—a stenographer. What a grotesque scene! And utterly impossible! Impossible if only for the simple reason that the ancient Greeks had quite a different kind of memory and did not need to rely on something as far removed from the world as the shapes of shorthand in order to remember what came to them through speech. You see from this that something exceedingly destructive constantly has to interfere with our cultural life. We need this destructive thing. In the whole of our cultural life we cannot possibly do without shorthand. But we should be aware that there is something destructive in it. What after all in our cultural life is this dreadful habit of taking everything down in shorthand? It is as though we were no longer able to adjust our proper rhythm between waking and sleeping and were to use our sleep time to carry on all kinds of things so as to implant in our soul life something that it no longer takes in naturally. With our use of shorthand we retain something in our culture that if left to ourselves with our present natural aptitudes we should cease to notice, should indeed forget. We thus keep something artificially awake in our culture that destroys it just as much as the nightly swotting of overzealous students ruins their health. Therefore our culture is no longer absolutely healthy. But we must realize that we have already crossed the Rubicon; that was in ancient Greek times. The Rubicon was crossed before which mankind had an absolutely healthy culture. Now our culture will become ever more unhealthy and man will more and more have to make out of the educational process a healing process against all the things that make him sick in his environment. We may not allow ourselves to indulge in illusions about this. And for this reason it is so boundlessly important to link writing to drawing and to teach writing before reading.

Then somewhat later we bring in arithmetic. Since there is no exact point in the development of the child when this must start, we can fit it in with other things that have to be considered. So, we start somewhat later with arithmetic. We shall build what belongs to this subject into the curriculum later, but we start in the manner I have described. And in this first stage the curriculum will always include a certain amount of foreign language lessons, for this is necessary from the cultural point of view. But for children of this age group foreign language lessons must only involve learning to speak, the children must learn to speak the foreign language.

Only in the second stage, from the ninth to about the twelfth year, do we start more to develop self-awareness. And we do this in grammar. Through the change he has undergone in the way I described it to you, the human being is now able to take into his self-awareness what can grow for him out of grammar. At this time we deal principally with word-inflections. Then we make a start with the natural history of the animal kingdom in the way I described with the cuttle-fish, mouse and human being. Later we let the plant kingdom follow, as you will be showing me this afternoon.[34]

During this stage of the child's development we can also make the transition to geometry, whereas before this stage whatever is later to become geometry is held within the bounds of drawing. With drawing we can develop the triangle, the square, the circle and the line for the child. The forms are developed through drawing in that we draw them and then say: This is a triangle, this is a square.—But the element of geometry that is added not before the ninth year is the search for the relationships between forms. Foreign languages continue of course and the more grammatical side is now introduced.

Lastly we introduce the children to physics. Then we come to the third stage leading up to the fourteenth, fifteenth years. We now start to teach syntax for which children are only really ready at about twelve years of age. Before that we treat in an instinctive way what can lead to the forming of sentences by the children.

The time has also come when using the forms of geometry we can embark on the mineral kingdom. We deal with the mineral kingdom by constantly linking it to physics, which we also now apply to man as I have said: refraction of light—the lens in the eye; we introduce both physics and chemistry. We now also make a start on history. Geography we can support by natural history through linking it with the concepts of physics and by geometry through the drawing of maps; we supplement geography with all this and finally show its connections with history. That is, we show how the different peoples have developed their characters.

This is carried on during the whole of these two stages in child development. Foreign languages of course still continue and can now be extended to include syntax.

Naturally a number of things will have to be taken carefully into consideration. We cannot of course start to take music with the little children if there are others in the same classroom who need absolute quiet because they are supposed to be learning something. So we shall have to do painting and drawing with the little ones in the morning and take music in the later afternoon, for instance. In other words we shall have to divide up the available space in the school so that one subject does not disturb another. For instance we cannot expect poems to be recited or speak about history if the little children in the next room are trumpeting. These things, too, are matters that are linked with the structure of the curriculum and in establishing our school we shall have to take careful account of such questions as what should be done in the morning and what in the afternoon. Now that we know the three stages of the curriculum we see that we have the possibility of taking account also of the greater or lesser aptitudes of the children. Naturally we shall have to compromise, but for the moment let me presume that our situation is ideal and then later I shall throw light on the curriculum of modern schools so that we can strike an adequate compromise. It will be good (speaking now of the ideal) to have less of a sharp differentiation between the classes within each stage than between the stages themselves. We shall imagine to ourselves that a uniform progression up the school can really only take place between the first and second and between the second and third stages. For we shall discover that the so-called less gifted children usually take longer to understand things. Thus in each year's age range in the first stage there will be the more capable pupils who grasp things sooner and digest them later, and the less gifted who have

difficulties at first but in the end also understand. We shall
certainly experience this and for this reason we should
refrain from making premature judgments as to which
children are particularly gifted and which are less so. I have
stressed before that we shall be having children in our school
who have already attended a variety of classes elsewhere.
Dealing with them will be all the more difficult the older
they are. But we shall to a very great degree be able to
remould what has been spoilt in them if only we make
sufficient effort. Thus after having carried out what we
stressed in connection with foreign languages—Latin,
French, English, Greek—we should lose no time in starting
to do something the children enjoy most of all: letting them
carry on conversations together in the appropriate language
while the teacher does no more than guide the process. You
will find that they take tremendous delight in conversing
together in the appropriate language while the teacher does
nothing except make corrections or at most guide the conversation. Thus for instance if one of them says particularly
boring things he might be diverted to something more
interesting. The teacher's presence of mind will have to
serve him particularly well here. You must really feel the
children before you as a choir whom you are to conduct,
though this must be done even more in an inward way than
is the case with the conductor of an orchestra.

Then you must also ascertain what poems and other
pieces the children have been taught previously and what
they remember so that you can draw these from their
memories like a treasure. To this treasure they have stored
in their memories you link whatever grammar and syntax
they need to catch up with; it is extremely important that
the children should retain what they have in their memories
in the way of poems and so on and that they can link to this
whatever rules of grammar and syntax they need to become
aware of later in learning the language. I have said already

that it is not good if the memory is maltreated through the writing down of the sentences used in grammar lessons for the purpose of learning rules. These sentences must be forgotten. But what is learnt through them must be linked with what the children have stored in their memories. In this way what they have in their memories will later help them gain an increasing command of the language. If they later want to write a letter in that language or talk to someone in it, they should be able to call to mind rapidly the good turns of phrase they have learnt in this way. Taking such things into account is part of the economy of teaching. When teaching foreign languages you have to know what holds up progress. If you read something aloud to your class while they follow the text in their books, this is nothing but time eliminated from their lives. It is the worst you could possibly do. The right way is for the teacher to relate freely whatever he wants to put across to the children or, if he wants to present a passage or poem verbatim, to speak it by heart without using a book; meanwhile the pupils do nothing but listen; they do not read the text as the teacher speaks. Then possibly they are asked to reproduce what they have heard without having read it first. This is important for foreign language teaching but need not be taken into account so much for lessons in the mother tongue. What matters very much with the foreign language is that the children should understand through hearing rather than through reading, that things should become intelligible for them through speech. Later, when all this has been done, the children can be allowed to take their books and read the passage. Or, if this is not expecting too much of them, they can be given for homework the task of reading what has been dealt with during the lesson. In foreign languages, too, homework should be restricted mainly to reading tasks. Any written work to be done should really be done at school. In foreign languages as little homework as possible should be given, and not till the later stages after the age of twelve; even then it should only deal with things that happen in real life such as writing letters, business correspondence and so on, that is, things that really happen in life. To have children in school writing essays in foreign languages on subjects that have nothing to do with life is a real malpractice in a higher sense. We should be content with letter writing, business correspondence and similar things. At most we can go beyond this by letting the children recount things that have happened to them and that they have experienced. Up to the age of fourteen such recounting of real happenings should be cultivated far more than free composition. Indeed free composition really has no place in school before the ages of fourteen, fifteen. What does belong in school up to that point is the narrative recounting of what the children have experienced and heard; they must learn to take this in, for otherwise they cannot participate in a right social way in the cultural process of mankind. Indeed educated people today do on the whole notice only half the world and not the whole of it.

You know that experiments are undertaken nowadays, particularly in the interests of criminal psychology. Everything has to be proved by experiment these days. Let me give you an example: A lecture is announced (these are academic experiments carried out at universities). For the purpose of the experiment you arrange beforehand with one of the students what will happen. You as the professor will mount the platform and utter the first words of your lecture. (All this is written down in great detail.) At that moment the student who is in the know leaps on to the platform and tears down the coat you have hung on a hook there. He does exactly what you have prearranged. You behave accordingly and make a rush at him to prevent him from taking down your coat. Still everything is prearranged. You wrestle, making the movements you have arranged beforehand. You have studied it in detail and learnt it by heart so that you do exactly as arranged. Then the audience, who of course are not in the know, will behave in some way. This you cannot prearrange. But perhaps you can try to take a third person into your confidence; it will be his task to observe exactly how the audience behave. And at the end of the experiment you get each individual member of the audience to write down what he has witnessed.

Such experiments have been made at universities. The very experiment I have just described to you has been made and the result was that out of an audience of about thirty people at most four or five reported the scene correctly! This can be verified because of course every action was prearranged and the scene was enacted accordingly. So hardly one tenth of the audience record the scene correctly. Most people write down the most absurd things when taken by surprise in this way. Nowadays, since we are so fond of experimenting, we do this kind of thing and then draw the important scientific conclusion that the witnesses who make statements in court are not reliable. For if of an educated audience in a university lecture hall (they are, are they not, all educated people) only one-tenth report correctly on an event while the others report incorrectly and some even put down utter nonsense, how can witnesses in court be expected to report correctly on something they have seen weeks or perhaps months ago? People with sound common sense certainly know this from life, for in the ordinary course of things people also tell you nearly always wrongly and hardly ever correctly about what they have seen. All you can do is develop a fine nose for detecting whether something is being told you rightly or wrongly. Of all the things people tell you from every side, hardly a tenth is true in the strict sense of being a report of something that has actually happened.

As a matter of fact people do things by halves. They

develop the half that they could more easily do without if they were to rely properly on sound common sense; it is the other half that is more important. We ought to see to it that our cultural life develops in a way that will mean that witnesses are more reliable and people tell more of the truth. But to achieve this we should start to work on it in childhood. That is the reason why it is so important to let children recount what they have seen and experienced rather than expect them to write free compositions. Then there will be inculcated in them the habit of telling in life, and perhaps also in court, not something they have invented but whatever is the truth as regards the external facts discerned by their senses. The will realm ought to be taken more into account in this than the intellectual element. The purpose of that experiment when the prearranged scene was enacted in a lecture hall and the statements of the audience were then taken down was to find out how many lies people tell. In an intellectual age like ours this is understandable. But we must bring our intellectual age back to the realm of the will. Therefore we must observe such educational details as that of letting the children, once they can write, and particularly after their twelfth year, recount events that have actually happened rather than cultivating free composition which really has no place in education before the age of fourteen or fifteen.

And it is especially important also to bring our pupils gradually to the point in foreign language lessons at which they are able to retell briefly something they have seen or heard. It will also be important to cultivate the element of reflex action in connection with language, that is, to give the children orders: Do this, do that—and make sure they carry them out. This exercise means that what the teacher speaks is not followed by reflection on what he has said or by a slow spoken answer, but by action. In this way the will realm, the element of movement, is cultivated in language lessons.

Once again these are things that you must ponder well and absorb and take especially into account in foreign language lessons. Our task will always be to unite the will realm with the intellect in the right way.

It will also be important to cultivate object lessons in our school, but without allowing them to become banal. The children should never have the feeling that what they are being told in an object lesson is really rather obvious. Here is a piece of chalk. What colour is it?—Yellow. What is it like at the top?—It is broken off.—Many an object lesson is given along these lines. It is atrocious. Something that is obvious in ordinary life should not be used as an object lesson. Such lessons should be lifted up to a higher level. When they are being given an object lesson the children should be transported by it to a higher sphere of their soul life. You can achieve this particularly well if you combine object lessons with geometry.

Geometry offers you an extraordinarily good example of how to link the object lesson with the subject matter itself. You start, for instance, by drawing a right-angled isosceles triangle for the children. Then below you attach a square to the triangle. So now we have a right-angled isosceles triangle with a square attached to it (diagram I). If you have not already done so, you teach the children that with an isosceles triangle the sides a and b are the two sides (cathetus) that contain the right angle and the side c is the hypotenuse. And on the hypotenuse you have constructed a square. All this refers of course only to an isosceles triangle. Then you divide the square with diagonal lines, colouring one part red (top and bottom) and one part yellow (right). Now you say to the children: I am going to cut out the yellow part and place it beside my drawing (diagram II).— Then you take the red part and attach it to the yellow. Now you have made a square to fit one of the two equal sides, but it is made of a red piece and a yellow piece. Thus your second drawing (diagram II) is the same size as what is yellow and red in the first drawing and amounts to half of the square on the hypotenuse. Now you do the same for the other of the two equal sides using blue and adding the blue piece at the bottom so that again you have a right-angled isosceles triangle. Again you cut it out (diagram III) so that now you have a square on the other of the two equal sides.

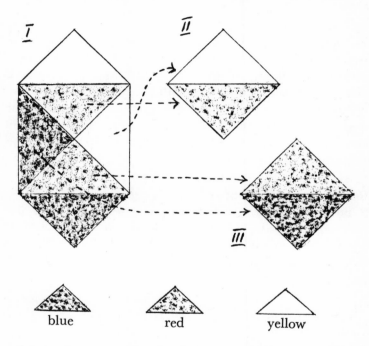

blue   red   yellow

Schopenhauer used to be furious in his day because the theorem of Pythagoras was not taught in this way and in his book *The World as Will and Idea* he expressed this in his rather course manner: How stupid schools are not to teach something like this by simply placing one part on top of another so that the children can see the actual demonstration of the Pythagorean theorem.—This in the first place

applies to isosceles triangles, but exactly the same can be
done with scalene right-angled triangles by fitting one part
over another in the manner demonstrated. That is an object
lesson. You can turn geometry into an object lesson. But
there is a certain significance (and I have often tested this
myself) when you aim to teach the children the Pythagorean
theorem after their ninth year, that you do so by planning
ahead how you will demonstrate it for them by fitting
together the parts of the square on the hypotenuse. If you as
the teacher are aware that you are aiming to do this in a
particular geometry lesson, you can in at most seven or eight
previous lessons teach them all the geometry that is necessary to lead up to the Pythagorean theorem, the well-known
'asses bridge'. It is very economical indeed to teach the
beginnings of geometry in this graphic manner. You will
save much time and you will also save the children from
something very significant (something that is destructive to
teaching if they are not saved from it), namely: You save
them from carrying out abstract thoughts in order to understand the Pythagorean theorem; you let them carry out
concrete thoughts and proceed from the simple to the
complex. You should start by fitting together the
Pythagorean theorem as shown here for the isosceles
triangle, and then you proceed to the scalene triangle. Even
when this is today done in the manner of an object lesson
(for it does happen sometimes) it is not wide enough to
cover the whole of the Pythagorean theorem; people do not
start first with the simple process of the isosceles triangle,
which is a good preparation, and then proceed to the
scalene right-angled triangle. But this is the very thing that
is important, quite consciously to include it in what the
geometry lessons are aiming for. What I beg you to consider
is the use of different colours. The various areas are treated
with colours which are then laid one on top of the other.

Most of you will have done something similar already, though not quite in this way.

I. Up to the ninth year
   music—painting, drawing
   writing—reading
   foreign languages; arithmetic somewhat later.

II. Up to the twelfth year
   grammar, word-inflections
   natural history of animal kingdom
   and plant kingdom
   foreign languages, geometry
   concepts of physics.

} geography

III. Up to the fourteenth year
   syntax
   minerals
   physics and chemistry
   foreign languages
   history.

LECTURE ELEVEN

Stuttgart, 2 September 1919

I have told you that geography is first introduced during the second of the three stages that fall between the ages of seven and fourteen. We can very well begin with it when the children have passed their ninth year. But it must be arranged in the right way. Indeed we must see to it that geography in future encompasses much more than it does at the moment for children up to fourteen, fifteen, and also for those over this age. It is too much pushed into the background these days and treated like the step-child of education. In geography the achievements of all the other lessons should meet and flow together in all sorts of ways. And though I have said that mineralogy is not taken up till the third stage, round about the twelfth year, it can in a narrative way, combined with direct observation, be woven into geography during the previous stage. Between the ages of nine and twelve children can take in an enormous amount from geography if only we go about teaching it in the right way. It is important particularly in geography that we should start with whatever the children already know about the face of the earth and about what takes place on the face of the earth. We endeavour in an artistic way to give the children a kind of picture of the hills and rivers and other features of their immediate surroundings. We work out with the children an elementary map of the immediate neighbourhood they are growing up in and therefore know. We try to teach the children what it means when you change your point of view from being within a neighbourhood to seeing it from outside, from the air; we go through the process with them of transforming a landscape into a map, taking at first the landscape they know. We endeavour to teach them how rivers flow through the district, that is, we actually draw the system of rivers and streams on the map into which we are transforming the neighbourhood. We also draw in the hills. It is good to work with colours, making the rivers blue and the hills or mountains brown. Then we add to the map the other things that are linked to the way people live. We put in all the configurations of the district, drawing the children's attention to them as we go: Here is a part where fruit trees are planted, so we draw in the fruit trees. Then we point out that there are also some

parts covered with coniferous trees, so we draw these in too.

We show them that another part of the neighbourhood is covered with cornfields, so these too must be included in our

map. There are also meadows to be added. This drawing

shows the meadows that can be mown. We point this out to

the children. Meadows that cannot be mown but do provide grass for the cattle, though it is shorter and sparser, are also included in our map. We tell the children that this is

pasture land. And so we bring the map to life for the children.

From this map they gain some sort of an overall view of the economic foundations of the neighbourhood. We also start pointing out to them that there are all sorts of things like coal and ore inside the hills. We show them how the rivers are used to transport things that grow or are made at one place to another place. We unfold for them much of what is connected with this economic structure of the district. Having made clear the economic foundation provided by the rivers and hills, fields and woods and so on, in so far as these things can be explained to the children, we next put in the villages or towns that belong to the district we are dealing with. And now we begin to point out why it is that a village appears at a particular place and how this is connected with the hills and what they might have to offer in their depths, and with the courses of the streams and rivers. In short, by using the map we endeavour to awaken in the children some idea of the economic links that exist between the natural formation of the land and the conditions of human life. This leads on to giving them a picture of the difference between country life and town life. We take

all this as far as the children are able to grasp it. And finally
we go as far as to show how man with his industry meets the
conditions nature offers him. That is we begin to show the
children that human beings make artificial rivers known as
canals, that they build railways. Then we point out how
with the help of the railways provisions can be transported
and how the very situation of people themselves in life is
affected. After having worked for a while towards an understanding of the economic relationships between natural
conditions and the conditions of human life, we can then
proceed to build on the concepts the children have gained
and lead them further into the world at large. If we have
taken the first steps in the right way it will not be necessary to be excessively pedantic in this. The pedant would say
at this point: The natural way is to begin with the geography of the immediate neighbourhood and then spread
out concentrically from there.—Even this is too pedantic.
There is no need to enlarge in this way. When a firm
foundation has been laid in the understanding of the links
between nature and man, we can quite well turn our
attention to something else. In the way we turn to something else, however, we should continue as effectively and
intensively as possible to develop the theme of the economic
links between man and his natural environment. Here in
our district, for instance, after developing the necessary
concepts from familiar stretches of land and helping the
children find their bearings in their own neighbourhood, we
can then widen their horizon by telling them about the
Alps. We now enter into the geography of the Alps. Having
already taught the children how to draw maps we can now
extend this by drawing a line showing where the Southern
Alps meet the Mediterranean Sea. You also draw the
Northern part of Italy, the Adriatic Sea and so on, saying:
There are great rivers here.—And you draw in the courses of
the rivers. You draw the Rhone, the Rhine, the Inn, the

Danube with their tributaries. And you add to the drawing the different arms of the Alps. The children will be extraordinarily fascinated when they discover how the different arms are separated by the rivers. Then along the blue lines of the rivers you can draw red lines, imaginary boundaries, for instance along the Rhone from the Lake of Geneva back to its source, and then along the Rhine, and further over the top of the Brenner and so on, dividing the Alps from West to East. You can then say: Look, down below I have drawn a red line along the rivers and at the top I have also drawn a red line. The Alps that lie between these red lines are different from those that lie above and below them. Now, and this is where mineralogy joins up with geography, you could show the children a piece of Jura limestone, saying: The mountain ranges above the top red line are made of limestone like this, and those under the lower red line also consist of it.—And for what lies in between you show them a piece of granite, gneiss, and say: These mountains in between the red lines are of rock like this, the oldest rock.— The children will be tremendously interested in this Alpine massif. You might perhaps also show them a relief map of the area that gives a more plastic impression of how the river courses divide the Alps into limestone Alps, gneiss, mica, slate and so on and how the whole length of the range is somewhat curved and shows from South to North the differentiation into limestone—granite—limestone, divided by the rivers. Without any pedantic object lessons you can bring much to all this that will greatly extend the children's range of ideas.

Then you go on (you have already prepared for this in your nature lessons) to describe to the children what grows down in the valley, what grows higher up the mountain side, what grows right high up, and also what at the very, very summit does not grow. You paint a vertical picture of the vegetation.

And now you begin to show the children how human beings establish themselves in a countryside dominated by its massive mountains. Help them picture to themselves a really high mountain village and how people must live there. Mark it on your map. Then you describe a village and the roads of a valley. And then the towns that appear at the confluence of a river with one of its tributaries. You describe in this wider context the relationship between the natural configuration of the land and the way man builds up his economic life. Out of the natural surroundings you in a way build up a picture of human industry, also drawing the children's attention again to the places where ore and coal can be found and how settlements are determined by such things.

Next draw for the children a picture of a landscape with no mountains, a flat plain, and treat this in a similar way. Describe the natural configuration, the structure of the ground and show them how some things grow on poor soil and others on rich soil. Point out to them how the soil is constituted on which potatoes grow (you can do this with quite simple means), or wheat, or rye and so on. You will already have taught them the difference between wheat, rye, oats. Do not hesitate to teach them things that as yet they can only understand in a general way and will only grasp more clearly in later lessons when they return to them from another point of view. Until they are twelve, introduce them chiefly to economic conditions and relations. Make these clear to them. And concentrate more on the geography of their own country than on giving them a complete picture of the earth. Let them, however, gain an impression of how vast the ocean is. You started drawing it when you showed where the Southern Alps meet the Mediterranean. Draw the sea as a blue surface. And draw the outlines of Spain and France and show how to the West there is an immense ocean. Then introduce gradually in a way that they can understand the idea that America also exists. They should have a mental picture of this before they are twelve.

If you start in this way with a good foundation, you can count on the children when they are about twelve having sufficient understanding for you to proceed more systematically, taking less time to give them a picture of the earth as a whole by teaching them about the five continents and also the oceans (more briefly than has been your method hitherto) and describing to them the economic life of these different continents. You should be able to draw everything out of the foundations you have laid. When, as I said, you have then drawn together in a picture of the whole earth all the knowledge about the economic life of man that you have given the children, you can, after having also taught them history in the manner described for about six months, transfer your attention to the cultural environment made by the people who inhabit the different continents. But do not take the step into this different sphere until you have made their souls somewhat adaptable by means of their first history lessons. Then you can also speak of the geographical distribution of the characteristics of the different peoples. Do not speak any earlier about the characteristic differences of the various peoples for it is only now that on the basis of the foundation I have described to you the children will bring their best understanding to this subject. You can now speak of the difference between Asiatic, European and American peoples, and of the difference between the Mediterranean peoples and the Northern peoples of Europe. Thus you gradually combine geography with history. You will be fulfilling a beautiful task and one that brings much joy to the children if you do what I have just described mainly between their twelfth and fifteenth year. You see that a great deal must be put into the teaching of geography so that it can really become a kind of summary of everything else we do with the children. And how much can flow together in geography! Towards the end a wonderful interplay between geography and history will be possible. Having put a great many things into your geography lessons you will then also be able to draw on them for a great many things. This will of course tax your imaginative abilities and your inventiveness. When you tell the children that here or there certain things are done, for instance that the Japanese make their pictures in such and such a way, you can then encourage them to do the same, albeit in their much more simple and primitive way. When you are telling the children about the links between agriculture and man's way of life, do not miss the opportunity of giving them a clear picture of a plough and a harrow in connection with the geographical picture. Let them also imitate some of the things you tell them, perhaps in the form of a little plaything or a piece of artistic work. This will give them skills and will fit them for taking their places properly in life later on. And if you could even make little ploughs and let them cultivate the school garden, if they could be allowed to cut with small sickles or mow with small scythes, this would establish a good contact with life. For more important than dexterity is the soul contact made between the life of the child and the life of the world. It is a fact that a child who has cut grass with a sickle or mown it with a scythe, a child who has drawn a furrow with a little plough, will turn into a different person from one who has not done these things. Quite simply the soul element is changed. Abstract lessons in manual skills are not really a substitute for this. Paper folding and laying little sticks should be actively avoided, for these things tend to unfit the child for life rather than fit him for it. It is far better to encourage him to do things that really happen in life than invent things for him to do that do not occur in life. By building up our geography teaching in the manner I have described we acquaint the children in the most natural way with the fact that human life is brought together from many sides in various ways. At the same time we take care to deal with things that they are well able to understand. Thus between the ninth and twelfth years we describe economic conditions and external matters in our geography lessons. From this we lead on to an understanding of cultural and spiritual matters pertaining to different peoples. And then while saving all the details for later we merely hint at what goes on in the rights sphere of the different nations, letting only the very first most primitive concepts peep through the economic and cultural life. For the children do not as yet have a full understanding for matters of the rights sphere. And if they are confronted with concepts from this sphere too early on in their development, their soul forces are ruined for the rest of their lives because such things are so abstract.

It is indeed a good thing if you can use the geography lessons to bring a unity to all the other subjects. Perhaps the worst thing that can happen to geography is for it to be regimented into a strictly demarcated timetable, which is something we anyway do not want.

We shall anyway arrange things so that each subject can be treated for a longer span of time. We take children into the school and work first of all towards teaching them to write. That is, we occupy the hours that we claim from them in the morning with painting, drawing, and learning to write. Our timetable will not stipulate the first lesson to be writing, the second reading and so on; we shall occupy ourselves with similar things for longer stretches at a time. Not until the children can write a little shall we move on to reading. Of course in learning to write they also learn to read a little; but these can be combined in an even better way. We appoint definite periods for the other things too, not following one subject with another, lesson by lesson, but staying with one subject for quite some time and only coming back to other things after several weeks. Thus we concentrate our lessons and are in a position to teach much more economically than would be the case if we had to waste our time and energy on adhering to some dreadful timetable, teaching a subject in one lesson and then wiping it out in the next lesson by teaching something quite different. Particularly with geography you can see how you can approach it from all sorts of directions. It is not laid down for you that you have to teach geography from the ninth to the tenth year; instead you are left free to decide when the time is ripe to fit geography in with whatever else you have been doing.

This of course imposes a great deal of responsibility on you, but without such responsibility no teaching can be carried out. A curriculum that from the start lays down the timetable and all sorts of other things completely eliminates the art of teaching. And this must not be. The teacher must be the driving and stimulating force in the whole educational system. What I have just shown you about the way to deal with geography teaching is an excellent example from which you can gain a proper picture of how everything should in fact be done. Geography really can become a great channel into which everything flows and from which a great deal can also be derived. You have, for instance, shown the children in the geography lesson how limestone mountains differ from granite mountains. Now you can show them a lump of granite or gneiss and point out how it contains different minerals including something that sparkles. Then you show them a piece of mica and tell them that what they see sparkling in the granite is mica. Then you can show them all the other substances hiding in granite or gneiss. You show them some quartz and try to unfold the whole mineral world out of a lump of rock. This is another good opportunity for adding a great deal to the children's understanding of how things that belong together as a whole can be divided into their separate parts. It is far more useful to teach them about granite and gneiss first and afterwards about the minerals they consist of than it is to start with the quartz, mica, felspar and so on and then show that they are all mixed up in granite or gneiss. Mineralogy is a very good subject for starting with the whole and moving to the parts, for starting with the way a mountain is constructed and moving on to mineralogy. And this certainly helps the children.

With the animal kingdom you will proceed in the opposite direction, building up from the individual animals. The plant kingdom, as we have seen in our seminar discussions,[35] is to be treated as a totality before we look at the details. And for the mineral kingdom nature itself often supplies us with the totality from which we can then proceed to the details.

Furthermore, again linking mineralogy with geography, we must not omit the discussion of how all the things of economic value that we find in nature are used. Referring to what we have said about the stony structure of the mountains, we then discuss all the things, such as coal, that we have a use for, in industry as well as elsewhere. We describe these things in a simple way, but our starting point is our discussion of the mountains.

Nor should we neglect to describe a saw-mill when we are dealing with the forest. Having started with the forest we next move on to a discussion of wood and come finally to the saw-mill.

We can do a tremendous amount in this direction if we do not have to start with a timetable that is laid down with military precision but can proceed in accordance with what arises out of the lessons. But we must have a good idea of what is required by the children in the different stages of their development from the time they start school up to their ninth year, from their ninth to their twelfth year, and from their twelfth to their fifteenth year.

LECTURE TWELVE

Stuttgart, 3 September 1919

We must not close our minds to the fact that man's relationship with his environment is far more complex than that
part of which we are always conscious. From very varied
points of view I have endeavoured to clarify for you the
nature and significance of the unconscious and subconscious
workings of the soul. In the sphere of education and educational method it is particularly important that human
beings should be brought up in a way that suits not only
their conscious being but also their subconscious and unconscious soul forces. To be a real educator and teacher you
cannot avoid entering into the subtleties of man's being.

We have come to know the three stages of human
development between the change of teeth and puberty. We
must be quite clear that, particularly in the last of these
stages, in addition to the conscious realm the subconscious
plays a large part, a part that is significant for the whole
future of the human being.

By looking at this matter from another point of view I
should like to make clear to you why this is so.

Just think how many people today travel by electric train
without having the faintest idea how an electric train is set
in motion. Imagine even how many people see a steam
engine rushing by without having any clue as to the workings of physics and mechanics that propel it. Consider what
position such ignorance puts us in as regards our relationship with our environment, that very environment we use
for our convenience. We live in a world that has been

brought about by human beings, that has been formed by human thoughts, that we use, and that we know nothing about. This fact, that we understand nothing about something that has been formed by man and is fundamentally the result of human thinking, is greatly significant for the whole mood of soul and spirit of mankind. Human beings literally have to turn a deaf ear in order not to perceive the effects that are resulting from this.

It is always very satisfying to notice how people (now I do not want to offend anyone with my turn of phrase) from the better classes enter a factory and feel thoroughly ill at ease. This happens because there shoots up from their subconscious the feeling that they use all the things that are manufactured in this factory without having the slightest relationship as human beings with what goes on there. They know nothing about it. When you notice the discomfiture of an inveterate cigarette smoker (to take a familiar example) as he enters the Waldorf-Astoria cigarette factory, knowing nothing about what goes on so that he can be kept supplied with his cigarettes, you can be pleased by the fact that at least he can still dimly perceive his ignorance about the environment born out of human thoughts, the environment in which he lives and of which he uses the products. We can be glad if people enter and leave an electric train with a slight feeling of unease because they have no idea how it works. For this sensing of discomfiture is the first beginning of an improvement in this realm. The very worst thing is to experience and live in a world made by human beings without bothering ourselves about this world.

We can work against these things only by starting during the last stage of the lower school, by really not letting the fifteen, sixteen-year-olds leave school without at least some elementary ideas about the more important procedures taking place in life. We should teach them in a way that leaves them with a yearning to be curious and inquisitive at every opportunity about what is going on around them so that they use this curiosity and thirst for knowledge to add to whatever they already know. Thus towards the end of the lower school we should employ all the different subjects in a comprehensive sense towards a social education of our pupils, just as we use the separate subjects in geography to build an overall geographical structure in the way I described in my previous lecture. In other words we must not neglect to use the concepts learned earlier of physics and natural history to introduce the children at least to the industrial processes closest to them. In their fifteenth or sixteenth year they should at least have gained some idea of what goes on in a soap factory or a spinning mill. Naturally we shall have to proceed as economically as possible. It is always possible to condense out of the overall complicated processes a simple, generalized picture. I think Herr Molt[36] will agree that one could teach children in an economical way about the whole process of cigarette manufacture from beginning to end in a few simple sentences that would then only need a little elucidation derived from the remainder of the subjects we have taught them. It is utterly beneficial for children in their thirteenth, fourteenth, fifteenth, sixteenth year to be given such condensed descriptions of different branches of industry. It would be very good if during these years they were to keep an exercise book in which to record the processes of soap manufacture, cigarette manufacture, spinning, weaving, and so on. They need not be taught about mechanical and chemical technology on a grand scale, but they would gain a great deal from keeping such an exercise book. Even if the book were later to be lost, a residue would remain. They would not only have the benefit of knowing these things, but, more important, they would feel as they went through life and their profession that they had once known these things, that they had once been through the process of learning about them. This affects the assurance with which a person acts; it affects the self-possession with which he takes his place in the world. It is very important for his will-power and his capacity for making decisions. No profession is without people of efficiency and initiative who occupy their place in the world with the feeling about the things they do not actually need for their own profession that they once knew about them, even if only in a primitive way. Even if they have forgotten it, something will still remain. However, we do learn a lot in school. And in object lessons, which so often degenerate into platitudes, such things are also taught to pupils. But in these cases it can be found that later no feeling remains that says: I once learnt about that and how fortunate I was to have done so.—Instead the feeling is: Thank God I have forgotten all that; what a good thing that I have forgotten what I learnt then.—We ought never to be responsible for arousing this feeling in a person. If in our childhood we were taught in a manner that took account of what I have just said, then when we later enter a factory or something similar, innumerable things will shoot up out of our subconscious. Today everything is specialized in life. This specialization is actually dreadful. And the main reason why so much in life is specialized is because we start to specialize already in the way we teach in schools.

The gist of these remarks might well be summarized in the words: Every single thing a child learns during the course of his schooling should in the end be presented so broadly that threads may everywhere be found linking it with practical human life. Very, very many things that are now unsocial in the world would be made social if we could at least touch upon an insight into matters that later need not have any direct bearing on our own work in life.

Thus, for instance, we ought to take careful note of what in the outside world is considered important in school subjects that are still rooted in older, good, though perhaps atavistic insights in teaching. In this connection I always want to point to a most remarkable phenomenon. When those of us who are now old started on our secondary school courses in Austria at the age of fourteen or fifteen, we had relatively good geometry and arithmetic textbooks. These have now disappeared. A few years ago in Vienna I hunted through all kinds of second-hand bookshops for older geometry textbooks because I wanted once again to have before my physical eyes what gave such delight to us boys, for instance in Wiener-Neustadt. On the day we entered the first class of the senior school, the boys from the second class met us in the corridor shouting: Fialkowskiy, Fialkowskiy, you'll have to pay up tomorrow!—Thus we pupils in the first class took over Fialkowskiy's[37] geometry textbook from the pupils of the second class and brought them the money the next day. And I actually found one of these Fialkowskiy geometry books during my hunt. It gave me a great deal of pleasure because it shows that much better geometry books for schools were written in the old tradition than was the case later. The present-day books that have replaced the older ones are really quite atrocious. And the situation in the field of arithmetic and geometry is particularly bad. But if we think back only a little to the generations before us, they certainly had better textbooks. These nearly all came from the school of the Austrian Benedictines. It was the Benedictine monks who had written the mathematical and geometrical books and these were very good because the Benedictine Order is the Catholic order that takes great care that its members should be taught very well in geometry and mathematics. The general conviction within the order is that it is ludicrous for someone to mount the pulpit and speak to the people if he does not know any geometry or mathematics.

This ideal of unity that fills the human soul must pulse through all teaching. Something of the world as a totality must live in every profession. And in particular there must be something there of whatever is opposite to the profession, something of what one thinks will be of hardly any use in that profession. One must occupy oneself with what is in a way the opposite of one's own profession. But one will only have the longing to do this if one is taught in the way I have described.

It was just at the time when materialism spread far and wide, in the last third of the nineteenth century, that this materialism also permeated education to such a degree that specialization came to be considered very important. Please do not subscribe to the belief that you will make the children idealistic if you avoid showing them during the last years of the lower school and the first of the senior school how what you teach them is linked with practical life. Do not imagine that they will be more idealistic in later life if during these years you have them write essays on all sorts of sentimental feelings about the world, on the gentleness of the lamb, the fierceness of the lion and so on, and on God-permeated nature. You do not have an idealistic effect on the children in this way. You will do far more, in fact, to cultivate idealism if you do not approach it so directly, so crudely. Why have people in recent times become so irreligious? For the simple reason that what is now preached is far too sentimental and abstract. People are irreligious now because the Church pays so little heed to divine commandments. For instance there is the commandment: Thou shalt not take the name of the Lord thy God in vain. If you heed this and refrain from mentioning the name Jesus Christ after every fifth sentence or talking about God's universal order, you are immediately criticised by those so-called church-minded people who would prefer to hear you mention Jesus Christ and God in every sentence. These church-minded circles are the very ones who regard as an irreligious attitude the meek and quiet spirit that seeks to be

inwardly penetrated by the divine and avoids uttering
'Lord, Lord' at every moment. And if what is brought to
human beings by teachers is permeated by this quiet, inwardly working godliness that is not carried sentimentally
on the tip of the tongue, the cry, resulting from wrong
up-bringing, is heard on every side: Ah, yes, he ought to
speak far more about Christianity and such things.—We must
take care in education not to drag everything learnt by the
children into sentimentality, especially in their thirteenth,
fourteenth and fifteenth years, but rather lead what we
teach them more towards the workings of practical life.
Thus, basically, no child ought to reach his fifteenth year
without having been led in arithmetic lessons to a knowledge
of the rules of at least the most simple forms of bookkeeping. Similarly the principles of grammar should, during
these years, lead not so much to the kind of essay depicting
man's inner life as though bathed in a porridge of sentimentality (for this kind of brew, a glorified version of the spirit
that reigns when people gather over their wine in the
evening or at coffee parties, is the kind of essay usually
expected of the thirteen to sixteen-year-olds) but rather to
business compositions, business letters. No child should pass
beyond his fifteenth year without having gone through the
stage of writing specimen examples of practical business
letters. Do not say that the children can learn to do this
later. Yes, by overcoming dreadful obstacles they can learn
it later, but only if they can overcome these obstacles. It is of
great benefit to the children if you teach them to let their
knowledge of grammar and language flow into business
compositions, business letters. There should be nobody
today who has not once upon a time learnt to write a decent
business letter. He may not need to apply this in later life at
all, but there really should be nobody who has not once
been encouraged to write a decent business letter. If you
satiate the children mainly with sentimental idealism

between the ages of thirteen and fifteen, they will later develop an aversion to idealism and become materialistic people. If you lead them during these years into the practical things of life, they will retain a healthy relationship to the idealistic needs of the soul, since these can only be wiped out if they are senselessly indulged in during early youth.

This is extraordinarily important and in connection with it even some external points about the structure of the lessons are of great significance. You know that as regards the way we teach religion we shall have to make compromises. As a result something that one day will fill the soul element of our teaching with a religious element cannot at present flow into the rest of our teaching. The fact that we have to compromise in this manner stems from the way religious bodies have adopted an attitude to the world that is inimical to culture. But even today, if only the religious bodies would for their part also make compromises with us, a good deal could flow from this religious instruction squeezed in among the rest of the lessons.[38] If for instance the religion teacher would condescend from time to time to include in his lessons something from another subject; if, for instance, in the midst of his religion lesson he were able to link what he was saying to an explanation of the steam engine, or something astronomical, or something quite worldly, the simple fact that it would be the religion teacher doing this would be immeasurably significant for the consciousness of the growing children. I am quoting you this extreme example because in the rest of our lessons we shall have to observe this method even though it can be employed only in a limited way in the teaching of religion. We must not allow ourselves to think pedantically: Now I am teaching geography, now I am teaching history and need therefore not bother about anything else.—No indeed. When we explain to the children that the word *sofa* came from the Orient during the Crusades, we shall see to it that we then

include in the history lesson a description of the way sofas
are manufactured. This will lead us on to other items of
furniture that are more occidental. In other words, we shall
extract something quite different from the so-called 'subject'
of our lesson. This method of teaching is immensely beneficial for the growing children because moving from one thing
to another in a way that connects one thing with another is
more beneficial than anything else for the development of
spirit and soul and even of body. You can actually say: A
child to whose delight the teacher suddenly tells about the
manufacture of sofas in the middle of a history lesson,
leading on perhaps to a discussion of Oriental carpet
patterns, all given in a way that gives him a real view of the
subject, will have a better digestion than a child for whom a
French lesson is just followed by a geometry lesson. The
child will be actually physically more healthy. Thus we can
well structure our lessons in this inwardly healthy way.
Nowadays most people suffer from all sorts of digestive
disturbances, abdominal disturbances that are to a great
extent the consequence of our unnatural teaching, because we
cannot adapt our teaching to the demands of life. The worst
in this respect are the upper-class young ladies' colleges. If
someone were to make a study of the connection between
the teaching in these upper-class young ladies' colleges and
the incidence of gynaecological illness, this would provide a
most interesting chapter of cultural history. We simply have
to draw attention to such things so that through avoiding
much of what has come to the fore quite recently some
healing may enter into this field. Above all one must know
that man is a complicated being and that what one wants to
cultivate in him often requires preparation first.

If you want to gather interested children around you in
order, in your religious fervour, to tell them about the
glories of the divine powers in the world, then if you do this
with children not specially selected but coming from here

and there, what you say will go in at one ear and out at the other and never reach their feelings. If, having written a business letter with a group of children in the morning, you have the same group again in the afternoon carrying in their subconscious what has been brought about by the business letter in the morning, then you are fortunate if it is now a matter of teaching them some religious concepts, for you yourself will have roused in them the mood that is now calling for its antithesis. Truly these things are not being put before you as matters of some abstract point of method but because they are of immense importance for life. I should like to know who has not, on going out into life, encountered the enormous amount of unnecessary work that is done. Businessmen will always agree when you say: Here is an employee in some firm; he is told to write a business letter to a related branch or to somebody who is to undertake some selling for the firm; he writes this letter and receives an answer; then he has to write another letter and receives a further answer and so on.—This wasting of time has gained much ground in business life today. We certainly proceed in an immensely uneconomical way in our public affairs today. You can feel this. Anyone endowed with ordinary common sense suffers real tortures if he glances at the copy file in any office. This is not because he has an aversion to the forms of address or the interests depicted there but because everything is expressed in the most impractical manner possible and because this file could be reduced to at least a quarter of its size. And the sole reason for this is that the schooling of the fourteen, fifteen-year-olds is not arranged in a suitable way. This mismanagement can simply not be made up for later in life, or if it can, then only by conquering almost insuperable difficulties. The opportunities missed during this period cannot even be made up for at the further education college, because the forces that develop at this time peter out and are no longer present in that form later. It is on these forces that you count when you depend on someone not just to concoct a letter superficially with only half his mind on the matter but to give it his full attention and formulate it carefully and clearly.

What matters during the first stage of the children's development from the time they come to school up to their ninth year is that we should be thoroughly immersed in the nature of the human being so that we teach entirely out of this. In contrast, the most important thing for the planning of the curriculum during the children's thirteenth to fifteenth years is that we teachers should be immersed in life, that we should be interested in life and sympathetic towards it, and that we should teach out of the reality of life. I had to say all this to you before going on to put together the ideal curriculum for you, after which we shall compare this ideal curriculum with the ones that will play a part in your teaching, for we are surrounded everywhere with the external world and its organization.

LECTURE THIRTEEN

Stuttgart, 4 September 1919

You have seen that in these lectures concerned with teaching methods we have gradually approached the insights that are to give us the actual curriculum. Now I have told you a number of times that as regards what already exists we shall have to reach a compromise as to what we take into our school and how we incorporate it. For we cannot as yet create in addition to the Waldorf School the rest of the social environment by which it ought to be surrounded. And so from our existing social environment influences will stream towards us that will again and again frustrate any ideal Waldorf curriculum we might work out. But we shall be good teachers in the Waldorf School only if we know how the ideal curriculum relates to our curriculum as it will have to be to start with because of the influence of our external social environment. Right at the beginning of their schooling most significant difficulties will arise for the children that we must therefore point out first, and then there will be other difficulties in the thirteen, fourteen, fifteen-year-old age-group. The problems we shall encounter with regard to the youngest children will come about because of course the outside world already has its curriculum. Such a curriculum stipulates all sorts of educational goals, and we shall not be able to risk letting our children reach the end of their first and second years at school without knowing what children being brought up and educated elsewhere will know. By the time they have reached their ninth year of age, the children educated by our method will have surpassed the others, but in the interim period it could happen that they would have to show to some external commission of enquiry what they have learnt by the end of their first year at school. Now the things that an external commission of enquiry would expect them to know are the very ones that it is not good for them to know. Our ideal curriculum would have other aims than the requirements of a commission of enquiry. So stipulations from the outside world will partly destroy our ideal curriculum. This is the position at the lower end of the Waldorf School. In the higher classes we shall be dealing with children coming to us from outside schools who will not have been taught by the methods that should have governed their education.

The chief mistake attendant today on the education of children between their seventh and fourteenth years is that they are taught far too intellectually. However much people may hold forth against intellectualism, the fact remains that the aims in schools are far too intellectual. So children will be coming to us who have a strong tendency to be like old men and women, who have much more of old age in them than children in their thirteenth or fourteenth year should have. This explains why, in such youth organizations as the Pathfinders and others, when young people today themselves call for reforms and stipulate how they want to be brought up and educated, they reveal such atrocious abstractions, that is, such senile attitudes. And just when our young people demand, as do the members of the Youth Movement, to be taught in a youthful manner, it is the principles of old age that they are asking for. We really do come across this. I myself experienced a very good example during one of these sessions of the Workers' Council for cultural affairs[39] when a young member of the Youth Movement or some other youth organization came forward. He began to read out his absolutely tedious abstractions about how youth demanded to be taught and educated. For some this was just too boring, for everything he said was so obvious and this very fact of being so obvious has something senile about it. The audience grew restless and the young speaker hurled into their midst: I declare that the older generations do not understand youth.—But the fact was that this youngster, still half a child, was too senile just because of a thwarted education and thwarted teaching.

This is what we shall have to take very much into account with the twelve to fourteen-year-olds who come to our school and to whom for the time being we are expected, so to speak, to give the finishing touches. Thus great problems arise for us at the beginning and end of the school years. We must try as much as possible to do justice to the ideal curriculum and we must do our utmost not to estrange the children too much from modern life.

Now in the very first school year the curriculum contains something rather disastrous. It is expected that the children should achieve the aim of reading as much as possible while little is required in the way of writing. Writing need only be started but reading must be brought to the stage during the first year where the children can at least read pieces both in Gothic[40] and Latin script that have been read with them or to them. They must be able to do this in both Gothic and Latin script, while relatively little is required in the way of writing. If we could educate in an ideal way, we should of course start with the forms in the manner discussed and then we should let the children gradually change the forms, which we have ourselves developed, into the forms of hand-written characters. We shall do this; we shall not allow ourselves to be prevented from starting with drawing and painting and then evolving the written letters from this drawing and painting. And only after this shall we proceed to the printed letters. When the children have learnt to recognize the handwritten letters we shall make the transition to printed letters. We shall make one mistake, however, because there will not be enough time in the first year to mould both the Gothic and the Latin scripts in this way and then go on to reading both the Gothic and the Latin scripts. This would overburden the first year of school too much. Therefore we shall follow the path from painting and drawing to writing the Gothic script, then make the transition from Gothic written to Gothic printed letters with simple reading. Then, without first deriving the Latin letters from drawing, we shall move directly from printed German to printed Latin letters. We shall work this out as a compromise: In order to do justice to true education we shall develop writing from drawing, but on the other hand so that the children can keep up with the requirements of the curriculum we shall also start them on elementary reading of texts in Latin print. This will be our task as regards writing and reading.

In these lectures on method I have already pointed out that when we have developed the forms of the letters to a certain degree we shall have to proceed more rapidly.

Then above all we must endeavour to cultivate during the first year as much simple speaking and conversation with the children as possible. We read aloud as little as possible but prepare ourselves so well that we can bring to them in a narrative way whatever we want to tell them. Then we seek to reach the point where the children are able to retell what they have heard from us. We avoid using passages that do not stimulate the imagination and make as much use as possible of passages that stimulate the imagination really strongly, namely fairy tales. As many fairy tales as possible. And having practised this telling and retelling with the children for a long time, we then start in a small way to let them give brief accounts of something they have themselves experienced. For instance we let a child tell us something he likes telling us about. With all this telling of stories, retelling, and telling of personal experiences we develop without being pedantic about it the transition from the local dialect to educated speech* by simply correcting mistakes the children make; at first they will make many mistakes, but later fewer and fewer. Through telling and retelling we develop in the children the transition from dialect to educated speech. We can do all this and in spite of it the children will have reached the desired goal by the end of their first year at school.

However, we do have to introduce something that really ought not to be included in this very first year of schooling because it weighs on the child's soul: We have to teach the children what a vowel is and what a consonant is. If we could follow the ideal curriculum we would not do this during the first year. But then an inspector might come at the end of the first year and ask the children what an *i* is and what an *l* is and they would not know that one is a vowel and the other a consonant. And then it would be said that this ignorance was the result of Anthroposophy. So we must make sure that the children can distinguish between a vowel and a consonant. We must also teach them what is a noun and what is an article. And here we find ourselves in a real dilemma, because according to the present curriculum we are expected to use the German and not the Latin expressions for grammatical terms, and so we ought to say 'gender word' instead of 'article'. I think it would be better in this case not to be pedantic and simply to continue to say 'article'. Now I have already given you some hints on how to help the children distinguish between nouns and adjectives. You help them to see how a noun refers to something that stands outside in space by itself. You endeavour to say to them: Let us take *tree! Tree* is something that remains standing in space. But look at a tree in winter, and again in spring and again in summer. The tree is always there, but it

* This is necessary in German-speaking countries because the dialects bear little relation to the written language.

looks different in winter than it does in summer, and different again in spring. In winter we say it is brown. In spring we say it is green. In summer we say it is many-coloured. These are its characteristics.—Thus we first teach the children to distinguish between what remains the same and the characteristics that change, and then we say: If we need a word to describe what remains the same, that is a noun; and if we need a word for what changes on the thing that remains the same, that is an adjective.—Then you teach the children the concept of activity: Sit on your chair. You are a good child. Good is an adjective. But now stand up and walk. You are doing something. That is an activity. The word you need to describe this activity is a verb.—Thus we endeavour to lead the child to the fact and then we make the transition from the fact to the words. In this way we shall be able to teach the children without doing too much damage what is a noun, an article, an adjective, a verb. The most difficult is to understand what an article is because the children cannot yet understand the relationship between the article and the noun. We shall have to flounder about rather in abstractions in order to teach the children what an article is. But they have got to learn it. And it is better to flounder in abstractions, since it is anyway something unnatural, than think up all sorts of artificial ways of making clear to the children the significance and nature of the article, which is anyway impossible.

In short, it will be a good thing for us to teach in full consciousness of the fact that we are bringing something new into teaching. The first school year will afford us plenty of opportunity for this. And during the second year, too, a great deal of this sort of thing will creep in. But there will be a great deal in the first year that is enormously beneficial for the growing child. It will encompass not only writing but also elementary primitive painting and drawing since we need these as our starting point for writing. We shall not only have singing during the first year but also start learning about music in an elementary way with the help of instruments. From the start we shall not only let the children sing but also lead them towards an instrument. This will benefit them a great deal. We shall teach them the first elements of listening to the relationship between notes. And we shall endeavour to hold the balance between the bringing out of the musical element from within through song, and listening to the tonal element from outside or the producing of notes through an instrument.

All these things, painting-drawing and drawing-painting, and also the finding of their way into the musical realm will be for us during the children's first year at school a wonderful element in developing their will, which is something almost totally removed from present-day schools. And if for these little children we can also lead over ordinary gymnastics into eurythmy, we shall be promoting their will development to a very special degree.

I have been handed a curriculum for the first year of schooling; it says:

Religion   2 lessons a week
German   11 lessons a week
Writing (no specified number of lessons, but it
    is taught at length in the German lessons)
Local Geography   2 lessons a week
Arithmetic   4 lessons a week
Singing and Gymnastics together 1 lesson a week.

We shall not do this, for if we did we should be sinning too much against the welfare of the growing children. Instead we shall arrange as far as is possible to have the singing and music, and also the gymnastics and eurythmy in the afternoon and all the other things in the morning; in moderation, until we think they have had enough, we shall practise singing and music and also gymnastics and eurythmy in the afternoon with the children. To set aside only one lesson a week for these things is quite ridiculous. This alone must prove to you how the whole of teaching today is aimed at the intellect.

During the first year of elementary school we are after all dealing with children who are only just six or a few months older. When they are this age we can quite well practise the elements of drawing and painting with them, and also of music, and we can also do gymnastics and eurythmy. But if we give them religion lessons in the style of today we are certainly not teaching them religion but merely giving them a form of memory training, which is about the only good thing that can be said about it. For it is utterly nonsensical to speak to six or seven-year-old children about the concepts that play a part in religion. All they can do is memorize them. Memory training is of course quite a good thing but we must be aware of the fact that with these concepts we are presenting to the children all sorts of things for which they have absolutely no understanding as yet.

There is something else written down here for the first year of school about which we shall think or at least act in a way that differs from the usual. During the second year it appears even more prominently as a separate subject: good penmanship. Since we shall let writing evolve out of paint-ing and drawing there will be no need for us to draw a distinction between poor penmanship and good penman-ship. We shall endeavour not to distinguish between bad writing and good writing and ensure that all our writing lessons are such (and this is possible despite the external curriculum) that the children always write well, so well that they need never distinguish between good penmanship and bad penmanship. And if we take pains to converse with the children for a long time and let them do plenty of retelling, making an effort ourselves to speak correctly, then we shall at first only have to introduce the matter of right or wrong spelling by making a few corrections without introducing the two as different aspects of learning to write.

In this connection we shall of course have to watch ourselves particularly carefully. We Austrians even have to cope with a particular difficulty as teachers, for in Austria we have in addition to dialect speech and educated speech also a third element and that is the special Austrian school speech. In this all the long vowels were pronounced short and the short vowels long.[41] But if when we converse with the children we take pains to pronounce long what is long and short what is short, sharp what is sharp, drawn-out what is drawn-out, and soft what is soft and watch carefully what the children do, correcting and getting them to speak properly all the time, we shall create for them the necessary foundation for correct spelling. During the first year we need not do much more than create the proper foundations for this. So with regard to spelling we can remain in the realm of speaking for as long as possible and only let this merge into actual correct spelling last of all. This is the kind of thing that must be taken into consideration when it is a matter of treating in the right way the children who stand at the beginning of their school life.

The children who come to us at the end of their time at school, the thirteen to fourteen-year-olds, come to us warped by too intellectual an education. Too much emphasis has been laid on their intellect in the way they have been taught. They have experienced far too little of the blessings of also having their will and feeling life developed. Consequently we shall have to make up for lost ground in these spheres just in these last few years. We shall have to seize every opportunity to try to bring will and feeling into what is merely intellectual by taking much that the children have absorbed purely intellectually and transforming it into something that also stirs the will and feeling. We can assume

with absolute certainty that the children who come to us at
this age will, for instance, have been taught the theorem of
Pythagoras wrongly and not in the right way that we have
discussed here. The question now is how we can contrive to
give the children not only what they have missed but
something more as well so that certain forces that have
already dried up and withered may be quickened anew to
whatever extent is still possible. So let us for instance
remind these children about the theorem of Pythagoras. We
say: You have learnt it; now tell me what it says. You see,
you have just told me the theorem of Pythagoras which is
that the square on the hypotenuse is equal to the sum of the
squares on the other two sides.—But we can be certain that
there is nothing in the soul of the children that ought to be
there as a result of learning the Pythagorean theorem. So I
now do something more. I show them the theorem in a
more pictorial form and also make clear how it has
developed. I let the picture arise in a quite specific way. I
say: Three of you, come up to the blackboard. Now the first
of you can cover this area with chalk; everybody watch to
make sure that he does not use more chalk than he needs in
order to cover the area. The second can cover this other
area with chalk, using another stick.—And now I say to the
boy or girl who has covered the square on the hypotenuse
with chalk: Look, you have used just as much chalk as the
other two put together. You have spread as much chalk on
this square as the other two together because the square on
the hypotenuse is the same as the sum of the squares on the
other two sides.—In other words I let him gain a picture
through the using of the chalk. He enters into it even more
deeply with his soul when he thinks about how some of the
chalk has been worn down so that it is no longer on the stick
but on the blackboard instead. Then I go a step further and
say: Now I am going to divide up the squares, one into 16
squares, the other into 9 squares and the other into 25. One

of you shall stand in the middle of each square and you imagine it is a field that you have to dig over. Those who have dug the 25 small squares in this big one have worked just as much as those in the one with the 16 small squares and those in the one with the 9 small squares put together. Through your work the square on the hypotenuse has been dug over and so has the square on each of the other two sides.—In this way I link the theorem of Pythagoras with

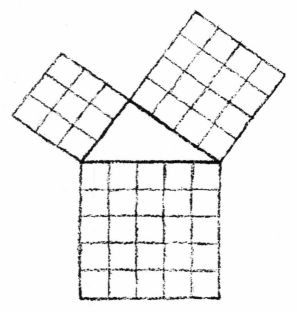

something that has a will influence in the children, something that at least lets them imagine themselves doing meaningful work with their will outside in the world; I bring to life something that they have got into their heads in a rather unliving way.

Let us now assume that these children have learnt Latin and Greek. I now attempt to bring them to the point where they not only speak Latin and Greek but where they also

listen, methodically, when one of them speaks Latin and
another Greek. And I try to bring vividly to life for them
the difference between the life of the Greek and the life of
the Latin. I should not need to do this in the ordinary
course of teaching, for it would come about of itself if the
ideal curriculum could be applied. But with the children
who come to us we need to do this because we must get
them to feel that when they speak Greek they speak only
with their larynx and their chest; and when they speak
Latin something of the whole human being always reverber-
ates with the langugage. The children's attention must be
drawn to this. Then I must also make them aware of the
living quality of French when they speak that, and how it
resembles Latin very closely. And how when they speak
English they almost spit out the sounds; the chest is less
involved than with the speaking of French; a very, very
great deal is cast off. Some syllables are literally spat out
before they have their full effect. You need not actually say
'spat out' to the children, but you must make them understand how just in English a word dies off towards the end.
In this way you endeavour to bring the element of articu-
lation particularly clearly into your teaching of languages
for the children in their thirteenth, fourteenth year who
come to you from present-day schools.

LECTURE FOURTEEN

Stuttgart, 5 September 1919

If you were to look back to the kind of curriculum still being issued quite recently, only fifty or sixty years ago, you would see that they were comparatively short. In a few brief sentences it was stated what was to be taken in the different subjects each year. Such a curriculum covered at most two, three or four pages; all the rest in those days was left to the actual practice of teaching, for this out of its own needs and its own powers was to stimulate the teachers to do what they should with the curriculum. Things are different today. The curriculum for secondary schools has swollen to the proportions of a book entitled 'Official Document'. And it not only stipulates what must be achieved but also contains all kinds of instructions on how to set about doing things in school. This means that during recent decades we have been in the process of letting education be swallowed by state legislation. Perhaps it is the dream of many a legislator gradually to bring out everything that used to be contained in the old literature on education as 'Official Publications' and 'Decrees'. Socialist leaders certainly have this impulse in their subconscious. Though today they are still ashamed to say so openly, it is certainly present in their subconscious; their ideal is to fetter in regulations what until comparatively recently still belonged to the domain of free spiritual life, also in the sphere of education.

For this reason we here, wanting as we do to preserve the educational system and teaching from the collapse which has overtaken it under Lenin and which could spread to

Central Europe, must approach an understanding of the curriculum in quite a different way from that in which ordinary teachers approach the 'Official Document'; they have taken it very seriously under the monarchy and during the era of ordinary democratic parliamentarianism, but they will view it with particularly servile feelings when it is sent to them by their dictator-comrades. The tyranny that can be inherent in socialism would be felt particularly strongly in the sphere of teaching and education. We have, then, to approach the curriculum in quite a different way. Our approach to it in fact has been such that we must put ourselves in the position of being able to create it ourselves at any moment, being able to read from the seventh, the eighth, the ninth, the tenth year of the child what we ought to do during these years. Tomorrow we shall juxtapose the ideal curriculum[42] and the curriculum that is at the moment customary in other Central European schools. We shall have prepared ourselves thoroughly for this conclusion if we have taken everything really into our feelings that we ought to have absorbed on our way to an understanding of the curriculum.

There is another exceptionally important aspect that is rather misjudged in today's official educational circles. At the close of my previous lecture[43] I spoke about the morality of education. This morality of education has to be put into practice during the actual lessons we give in the classroom. But it can only become actual practice in the classroom if one avoids a great deal of what is given in the way of examples in books on teaching practice. These books speak about object lessons. In itself there is nothing wrong with these and we have already discussed how such lessons should be conducted. Again and again, however, we have had to stress that they must never be allowed to sink into triviality, that they should never exceed a certain limit. The eternal cross-questioning of the pupils on self-evident things in

object lessons spreads a pall of boredom over the lessons that
ought not to be there. It deprives the lessons of the very
thing I stressed as being so important at the end of my
lecture an hour ago: the development of the children's
imaginative capacity. Speaking comparatively, if you discuss
with your pupils the shape of some saucepan or other by
way of an object lesson, you will undermine their imaginative faculty. But you will do a great deal better than what
often passes as an object lesson today if you discuss with
them the shapes of a Grecian urn and leave them to carry
over their own soul forces to an understanding also of an
ordinary trivial cooking pot. Object lessons as they are given
today often literally stifle the imagination. And it is not at
all bad if in teaching you leave a good deal unsaid so that
the children are induced to occupy themselves further in the
forces of their soul with what they have absorbed during
lessons. It is not at all good to want to explain everything in
the lesson down to the last dot on the i. If you do so, the
children leave school with the feeling that they have learnt
everything already and are on the lookout for some other
tomfoolery. On the other hand if you sow seeds for the
children's imagination, they remain fascinated by what they
have been offered during the lessons and are less inclined to
seek out some other tomfoolery. That our children today
turn into such rascals is connected solely with the fact that
we give them too much of the wrong kind of object lesson
and too little proper training for their feelings and their will.

There is still another way in which it is necessary for our
souls to become very intimately linked with the curriculum.

When you receive a child during the early years of school
he is quite a different being from the same child in his
thirteenth, fourteenth, fifteenth year. During the early years
of school the child is very, very much a bodily being, he is
still very much immersed in his body. When the time comes
for him to leave school in his fourteenth, fifteenth year, you

must have implanted in him the capacity no longer to
cling to his body with all the fibres of his soul but to be
independent of his body in thinking, feeling and willing.
If you endeavour to immerse yourselves somewhat more
profoundly in the nature of the growing human being, you
will find that during the early years of school he will still
possess relatively healthy instincts, particularly if they have
not been spoilt during the very early years. During the early
school years children do not yet have such a craving to stuff
themselves with sweets and suchlike things. They still have
certain healthy instincts with regard to food just as an
animal, because it is completely immersed in its body, has
very good instincts with regard to its food. The animal, just
because it is right inside its body, avoids what is bad for it.
At least it is certainly an exception in the animal world for
an evil to spread in the way alcohol has spread in the
world of human beings. The spread of such evils as alcohol
is due solely to the fact that the human being is such a
spiritual being and can become so independent of his physical nature. The physical body is far too sensible, for
instance, ever to be tempted to become an alcoholic. So,
relatively healthy instincts regarding food still live in children during the early years of school. For the sake of the
individual's development these instincts fade away during
the thirteenth, fourteenth, fifteenth years. And when puberty finally overtakes the child this also means that he has
lost his good instincts with regard to food, that he has to
replace with reason what his instincts gave him during
earlier years. This is why you can, as it were, intercept the
last manifestations of the growing child's instincts for food
and health during his thirteenth, fourteenth, fifteenth years.
You can still just catch the tail end of his healthy instincts
for food, for growth and so on. Later you can no longer
reach an inner feeling for proper nutrition and health care.
Therefore during these years the children must receive in

school some instruction on nutrition and health care for the human being. This is the very subject for object lessons. Object lessons here can very well support the imaginative faculty. Show to the children (or remind them that such things exist, for they will have seen them before) some substance that consists mainly of starch or sugar, a substance that is chiefly fat, and a substance composed mainly of protein. The children know this. But remind them that it is in the main from these three ingredients that the activity of the human organism proceeds. Taking this as your point of departure, you can during these years explain to the children the mysteries of nutrition. Then you can exactly describe to them the breathing process and develop for them everything related to the care of the human being's health with regard to nutrition and breathing. You will gain enormously for the way you educate and teach by giving this instruction just during these years, for you then catch the last instinctive manifestations of the instincts for what is health-giving and nutritious. This is why you can teach children about conditions of nutrition and health during these years without making them egoistic for the whole of their later life. It is still natural for children of this age to fulfil their health and nutritional needs instinctively. Therefore you can speak about the subject and what you say is met by something that is natural to the human being and does not make him egoistic. If children are not taught about the conditions of health and nutrition during these years, they have to inform themselves on this later by reading or from the information others give them. And what comes to a person after puberty, by whatever means, with regard to the conditions of nutrition and health, produces egoism in him. It is entirely unavoidable that it should produce egoism. If you read about nutritional physiology, if you read a summary of the rules of health care, you make yourself more egoistic than you were before; this is inherent in the very nature of this subject. This egoism that constantly originates in our becoming acquainted through reason with the way we have to take care of ourselves, this egoism has to be combatted with morality. If we did not have to care for ourselves physically, we should need no morality in our soul. But a person is less exposed to the dangers of egoism later in life if he has been taught about nutrition and health care during his thirteenth, fourteenth year when such instruction does not yet make for egoism but for what is natural to the human being.

You see to what a high degree the very questions of life are embedded in the right moment for teaching different things to human beings. You really make provision for the whole of life if you teach the human being the right things at the proper time. It would of course be best of all if we could teach the seven and eight-year-olds about nutrition and health care. Then they would absorb the knowledge about nutrition and health in the most unegoistic way, because they still hardly know that it refers to themselves. They would regard themselves as an object and not as a subject. But they cannot understand enough yet; their power of judgment has not developed sufficiently for them to understand. Therefore we cannot teach them the subjects of nutrition and health care during these early years but must save them up for their thirteenth or fourteenth year when the fire of their instinct for nutrition and health is beginning to fade but when the fading of this instinct is compensated for by the presence of the capacity to comprehend something that is to be considered. With the older children there will be every possibility of mentioning almost as an aside many things that relate to health and nutrition. In natural history, in physics, in lessons that expand on geography, even in history, it will be possible to bring in matters relating to nutrition and health care. You will see from this that it is not necessary to include these things as a subject in the timetable and that much must live in the lessons in a way that enables us to let it mingle with the other subjects we teach. If we have an understanding of what the child ought to be taking in, then he himself, or the whole community of children gathered in the school, will tell us daily what we ought to be including by way of interspersed remarks in our lessons and how just because we are teachers we have to develop a certain presence of mind. If we have been drilled as subject teachers for geography or history, then we shall not develop this presence of mind, for our aim then will be to do nothing but history from the beginning of the history lesson to the end. Then those exceptionally unnatural conditions are created of which the damaging effects on life have not even been fully considered as yet.

It is an intimate truth that we benefit a human being, we do something that prevents his egoism from developing too much, if we teach him about nutrition and health care during his thirteenth or fourteenth year in the way I have described to you.

Also, now, it is possible to point to many things that can permeate with feeling the whole way we teach our lessons. And if you attach something to do with the feelings wherever you can to your subject matter, then what you want to achieve in your teaching remains with the pupils for the rest of their lives. But if during the thirteenth, fourteenth, fifteenth year you teach only what appeals to reason and intellect, not much will remain with them for life. Therefore it must be your intention to permeate with feeling in your own being whatever you give in an imaginative way during these years. You must endeavour to put forward geography, history, natural history during these years in a vivid and graphic way that is nonetheless filled with feeling. To the imaginative element must be added the feeling element.

Thus, with regard to the curriculum, the time from the

children's seventh to their fourteenth, fifteenth year does indeed fall clearly into the three parts with which we have been concerning ourselves. First up to the ninth year when we bring to the growing child mainly the conventional elements, writing and reading; then up to the twelfth year when we bring to the growing child everything that is derived from the conventional but on the other hand comes also from what is founded in the human being's own power of judgment. As you have seen, during this period at school we study the animal kingdom and the plant kingdom because at this age the children still have a certain instinctive feeling for the relationships that play into these things. I have shown you during our lectures on teaching methods how you should develop a feeling for the relationship of man with the whole world of nature—cuttle-fish, mouse, lamb and human being. We have also made a great effort (which I hope will not be in vain, for it will bear flowers and fruit during the botany lessons) to develop a feeling for man's relationship with the plant world. These things should be developed through mental pictures filled with feeling during this middle period while the children's instincts of feeling themselves related with the animals and the plants are still present and while, after all, even if not with the ordinary light of reasoning consciousness, the human being easily feels himself at one moment to be a cat, and at the next a wolf, a lion, an eagle. This feeling of being first one creature and then another is still present only just after the ninth year. Before that it is stronger but it cannot be penetrated because the necessary power to grasp it is non-existent. If children were very precocious and talked about themselves a great deal in their fourth and fifth years, they would very, very frequently be comparing themselves with an eagle, a mouse and so on. But if in their ninth year we set about teaching them natural history in the way we have indicated, we shall still come upon a great deal of related, instinctive feeling in the children. Later this instinct matures so that there is also a feeling of being related with the plant world. Thus we first teach the natural history of the animal kingdom and then the natural history of the plant kingdom. We keep the minerals till the last because for them almost nothing but the power of judgment is necessary and this does not call upon anything through which man is related to the outside world. And man is indeed not related with the mineral kingdom. It is the mineral kingdom more than any other that he has to dissolve, as I have shown you.[44] Man does not even tolerate undissolved salt in his organism; as soon as he takes it in he has to dissolve it. It lies, then, very much within the nature of the human being to arrange the curriculum in the manner suggested. There is a beautiful balance in this middle period from the ninth to the eleventh year between instinctive powers and the power of judgment. We can always be sure that the child will meet us with understanding if we count on a certain instinctive comprehension and if we do not, particularly in natural history and botany, describe things too graphically. We must avoid external analogies particularly with reference to the plant world, for this really does go against the grain of natural feeling. Natural feeling is in itself predisposed to seek for qualities of soul in plants; not the external physical form of man in this or that tree but soul relationships such as we have just tried to discover[45] in the plant system.

And the actual power of judgment that lets us count on reasoned, intellectual understanding belongs to the last of the three periods. That is why we use the twelfth year, when the child is moving towards an understanding based on judgment, in order to let this merge with what still requires some kind of instinct, even though this is already strongly overshadowed by the power of judgment. Here we find the twilight instincts of the soul that have to be overcome by the power of judgment.

We must take into account that during this stage the human being has an instinct for the calculation of interest rates, for what can be raked in as profit, for the principle of discount and so on. This appeals to the instincts; but we must let the power of judgment be much stronger than this, so during this period we must deal with the relationships that exist between the element of calculation, the circulation of commodities and the ownership of property and wealth, in other words percentage and interest calculations and so on, discount calculations and similar matters.

It is exceedingly important that we should not teach the children these concepts too late. If we teach these concepts too late it means that we can count only on the children's egoism. We do not yet reckon with egoism if towards their twelfth year we teach them something about the concept of the bill of exchange and so on and about the concepts of commercial calculation. Actual bookkeeping can then be taken later; it has more reasoning in it. But to teach them these concepts is very important for them at this age. For the inner selfish feelings for interest rates, bills of exchange and so on are not yet stirring in children who are so young. Later in commercial college when they are older this is rather more serious.

Such are the things that you as teachers must take into yourselves very fundamentally. Please do try not to overdo things, for instance when you are describing the plants. You should endeavour particularly in plant lessons to teach in a way that leaves a great deal to the children's imagination, so that out of their own feelings they can form imaginatively very much about the soul connections between the human soul and the plant world. Those who enthuse too much about object lessons just do not know that the human being also has to be taught about some things that simply are not visible externally. And if we endeavour to teach human beings by means of object lessons certain things that we ought to teach them through working on them in a moral and feeling way, we do them actual harm through the object lessons. We must not forget that the mere observation and demonstration of things is very much a by-product of the materialistic views of our age. Of course observation should be cultivated in its proper place, but it is wrong to transform into observation what is more suitable for letting a moral and feeling influence work from teacher to pupil.

Now I believe you have taken in enough to make it really possible for us to form our curriculum.

With these words Rudolf Steiner brought to an end his lectures on 5 September 1919.

On the following day in the three curriculum lectures[46] he gave an outline of the aims of teaching in the different subjects during the different ages of the children in the various classes; he pointed to the subjects that can be linked together in the way they are treated.

At the close of this fortnight's work with the teachers Rudolf Steiner then spoke the following words:

CLOSING WORDS*

Today I would like to conclude these discussions by drawing your attention once more to something which I wish to lay upon your hearts. And that is that I would like you to keep steadfastly to the following four principles:

Firstly, the teacher must see to it that he influences and works upon his pupils—in a wider sense by letting the spirit flow through his whole being as a teacher, and also in the details of his work, how he utters each single word, or develops each individual concept or feeling. The teacher must be a man of initiative. He must be full of initiative. He must never be careless or lazy; at every moment he must stand in full consciousness of what he is doing in the school and how he behaves to the children. This is the first principle. *The teacher must be a man of initiative in everything that he does, great and small.*

Secondly, my dear friends, we as teachers must be interested in everything that is going on in the world and in all that concerns mankind. All that is happening in the outside world and in the life of men must arouse our interest. If we as teachers were to shut ourselves off from anything that might interest human beings, it would be a deplorable thing. We should take an interest in the affairs of the outside world, and we should also be able to enter into all the concerns, great or small, of every individual child in our care. That is the second principle. *The teacher should be one who is interested in the being of the whole world and of humanity.*

Thirdly, *the teacher must be one who never makes a compromise*

* Also included in the volume *Discussions with Teachers*. Translated by Helen Fox.

199

in his heart and mind with what is untrue. The teacher must be one who is true in the depths of his being. He must never compromise with untruth, for if he did so we should see how through many channels untruth would find its way into our teaching, especially in the way we present our subjects. Our teaching will only bear the stamp of truth if we are intently striving after truth in ourselves.

And now comes something which is more easily said than done, but which nevertheless is also a golden rule for the teacher's calling. *The teacher must never get stale or grow sour.* Cherish a mood of soul which is fresh and healthy! No getting stale and sour! This must be the teacher's endeavour.

And I know my dear friends that if during this fortnight you have received rightly into your inner life what we have been able to throw light upon from the most diverse points of view, then indirectly, through the realms of feeling and of will, what may still seem remote will draw very near to your souls as you work with the children in the classroom. During this fortnight I have only spoken of what can enter directly into your practical teaching, if you allow it first to work rightly within your own souls. But our Waldorf School, my dear friends, will depend upon what you do within yourselves, and whether you really allow the things which we have been considering to become effective in your own souls.

Think of the many things I have tried to make clear in order to come to a psychological conception of the human being, especially of the growing human being. Recall these things to your minds. And maybe there will come moments when you feel uncertain how or when to bring one thing or another into your teaching, or in what place to introduce it, but if you remember rightly what has been brought before you during this fortnight then thoughts will surely arise in you which will tell you what to do. Of course many things

ought really to be said many times over, but I do not want
to make you into teaching machines, but into free independent teachers. All that was spoken of during the last fortnight was given to you in this same spirit. The time has been
so short that for the rest I must simply appeal to the
understanding and devotion that you will bring to your
work.

Turn your thoughts again and yet again to all that has
been said which can lead you to an understanding of the
human being and especially of the child. It will be of service
to you in all the many questions of method which may
arise.

If you look back in memory to these discussions, then our
thoughts will surely meet again in all the different impulses
which have come to life during this time. For I myself, I can
assure you, shall also be thinking back to these days. For this
Waldorf School is indeed at this time weighing heavily on
the minds of those who are taking part in its inception and
organization. This Waldorf School must succeed. Much will
depend upon its success. Its success will bring a kind of proof
of many things in the spiritual evolution of mankind which
we have to represent.

If you will allow me in conclusion to speak personally for
a moment I should like to say: For myself this Waldorf
School will be a veritable child of care. Again and again I
shall have to come back to this Waldorf School with anxious
caring thoughts. But if we bear in mind the deep seriousness
of the situation we can really work well together. Let us in
particular keep before us this thought which shall truly fill
our hearts and minds: That bound up with the spiritual
movement of the present day are also the spiritual powers
that guide the Universe. If we believe in these good spiritual
powers, then they will be the inspirers of our lives and we
shall really be enabled to *teach*.

NOTES

Preface by Marie Steiner to the first edition in book form of this lecture course (1932): 'It will be our task to find teaching methods that always engage the whole human being.' With these words, Rudolf Steiner himself indicates the fundamental character of what he wanted to bring in this present course of lectures. Together with the lectures published under the title *Allgemeine Menschenkunde als Grundlage der Pädagogik (Study of Man)* they constitute an organic whole. The lectures that Rudolf Steiner gave in August and September 1919 to the first teachers of the Stuttgart Waldorf School, and a number of personalities who wanted to work in accordance with his educational principles, comprised three daily sessions. First thing in the morning came the lectures on the *Study of Man*; these were followed later in the morning by the present *Practical Advice to Teachers*; and the afternoons were devoted to seminar work with discussions.

The lectures *Study of Man. General Education Course* given in Stuttgart from 21 August to 5 September 1919 were published in a revised English translation by Rudolf Steiner Press, London, in 1966. The seminar work was first published in an English translation under the title *Discussions with Teachers* by Rudolf Steiner Press, London, in 1967.

1 In the original German this book is entitled *Grundlinien einer Erkenntnistheorie der Goetheschen Weltanschauung*. Published as *A Theory of Knowledge Implicit in Goethe's World Conception* by Anthroposophic Press, New York, 1940.

2 See *Wege zu einem neuen Baustil*. English *Ways to a New Style in Architecture*, Lecture One, Anthroposophical Publishing Company, 1927.

3 See *Study of Man*, Lecture II.

4 Johann Friedrich Herbart (1776–1841). *Allgemeine Pädagogik*, 1806, New Edition 1910; *Umriss pädagogischer Vorlesungen*, 1835, New Edition 1910.

5 See *Discussions with Teachers*, Discussion I.

6 Ways of dealing with the temperaments of children were discussed. See *Discussions with Teachers*, Discussion I.

7 See *Study of Man*, Lecture II.

8 Heinrich Heine (1797–1856). Son of Jewish parents. One of the greatest German lyric poets; also an outstanding satirist and publicist.

9 See Rudolf Steiner: *Die Kernpunkte der sozialen Frage in den Lebensnotwendigkeiten der Gegenwart und Zukunft*. First published in English as *The Threefold Commonwealth*. Latest (edited) edition in English: *The Threefold Social Order*, Anthroposophic Press, New York, 1972.

10 Johann Wolfgang von Goethe (1749–1832). See *Entwurf einer Farbenlehre, 6. Abteilung: Sinnlich-sittlicher Wirkung der Farbe* in the third volume of Goethe's scientific writings, edited and annotated by Rudolf Steiner, Troxler-Verlag, Bern, 1947. *A Theory of Colours* republished by John Murray, London, in 1967, is a translation of an earlier edition, not of that edited by Rudolf Steiner.

11 See Rudolf Steiner: *Über das Wesen der Farben*. English: *Colour*, Rudolf Steiner Press, 1971.

12 See Rudolf Steiner: *Ways to a New Style in Architecture* and *Der Baugedanke des Goetheanum*, Verlag Freies Geistesleben, Stuttgart, 1958 (not translated).

13 Tatjana Kisseleff (1881–1970), eurythmy teacher at the Goetheanum from 1914 to 1927, then stage eurythmist at the Goetheanum.

14 *The Merchant of Venice*, Act V, Scene I.

15 See Rudolf Steiner: *Eurythmie als Impuls für künstlerisches Betätigen und Betrachten*, 15 introductions to eurythmy performances (not translated).

16 Friedrich Schiller (1759–1805).

17 See Rudolf Steiner: *Inneres Wesen des Menschen und Leben zwischen Tod und neuer Geburt*. English *The Inner Nature of Man and Life Between Death and a New Birth*, Rudolf Steiner Press, 1959.

18 These suggestions have been taken up by the music teacher Paul Baumann. See his *Lieder der Freien Waldorfschule* (not translated).

19 See *Study of Man*, Lecture IV.

20 Rudolf Steiner is referring to experiences he had during the lectures on the threefold social order that he was giving in Germany at that time.

21 Novalis (1772–1801). Real name Friedrich von Hardenberg. In 1795 he became engaged to 14-year-old Sophie von Kühn. She died two years later and in 1800 Novalis wrote the six prose poems interspersed with verse, *Hymns to the Night*.

22 Ernst Meumann (1862–1915), a pupil of Wundt. Founder of experimental pedagogy. *Vorlesungen zur Einführung in die experimentelle Pädagogik*, 1907.

23 Arthur Schopenhauer (1788–1860). German philosopher, exponent of a metaphysical doctrine of the will. Principal work: *Die Welt als Wille und Vorstellung*, 1819. English translation *The World as Will and Idea*, 1883.

24 See *Discussions with Teachers*, Discussion VI.

25 Karl Julius Schröer (1825–1900). Literary historian; from 1867 professor at the Technical University of Vienna. Published inter alia *Deutsche Weihnachtsspiele aus Ungarn*, 1858, English translation by A. C. Harwood *Christmas Plays from Oberufer*, Rudolf Steiner Press, 1973.

26 Jean Paul (1763–1825). Real name Jean Paul Friedrich Richter.

27 See *Discussions with Teachers*, Discussion VII.

28 See *Study of Man*, Lecture VII.

29 See *Study of Man*, Lecture IX.

30 Franz von Miklosič (1813–1891). Famous scholar of Slav languages.

31 Franz Brentano (1838–1917).

32 Anton Marty (1847–1914). Pupil of Franz Brentano.

33 See *Discussions with Teachers*, Discussion VIII and following.

34 See *Discussions with Teachers*, Discussions IX, X and XI.

35 See *Discussions with Teachers*, Discussions IX, X and XI.

36 Emil Molt (1876–1936). Founder of the Free Waldorf School in Stuttgart in 1919. He and his wife as 'school father' and 'school mother' participated in the lectures to teachers. Frau Molt also taught handwork.

37 Nikolaus Fialkowskiy, architect and professor for geometry and geometrical drawing at the Vienna 'Communal-Realschule'. The book referred to is his *Lehrbuch der Geometrie und des Zeichnens geometrischer Ornamente*, J. Klinkhardt, Vienna and Leipzig, 1882 (not translated).

38 In Germany at the time of the founding of the Waldorf School and in some cases still today, parents could choose to have their children given religious instruction either by Catholic or Protestant clergy or by a member of the teaching staff. The latter gave the so-called 'free religion lessons'.

39 Workers' Councils of all kinds were set up in Germany after the First
World War.

40 Many Gothic characters differ totally from those of the Latin
alphabet. Both scripts were used in Steiner's day.

41 Translator's note: The following passage has been omitted from the
body of the text.
If the dialect said 'Sun' (the sun) and educated speech 'Sonne',
school speech said 'Sohne'. You cannot help getting into the habit of
this. You constantly fall back into doing it, just like a cat falling on
to its paws. It is very upsetting for the teacher too. And the further
South you go the worse it gets, till it reaches its very worst in
Southern Austria. If dialect speech says 'Su' (the son), school speech
says 'Son'. So you end up saying 'Son' instead of 'Sohn' for the boy
and 'Sohne' instead of 'Sonne' for what shines in the heavens. This is
only the most extreme case.

42 On 6 September 1919 Rudolf Steiner gave the three so-called
Curriculum Lectures. These have not been published in English, but
based on them are the books *Curriculum of the First Waldorf School*, by
C. von Heydebrand, Steiner Schools Fellowship, 1966, and *Rudolf
Steiner's Curriculum for Waldorf Schools*, by E. A. Karl Stockmeyer,
Steiner Schools Fellowship, 1969.

43 See *Study of Man*, Lecture XIV.

44 See *Study of Man*, Lecture XII.

45 See *Discussions with Teachers*, Discussions IX, X and XI.

46 See note 42.

List of relevant literature, published or distributed by Rudolf Steiner Press, except where otherwise stated, though not necessarily all in print at any one time:

By RUDOLF STEINER

Study of Man
Discussions with Teachers
    The above two titles are companion volumes to the present one.
A Modern Art of Education
The Kingdom of Childhood
Human Values in Education
The Spiritual Ground of Education
The Essentials of Education
The Roots of Education
The Education of the Child
Education as a Social Problem

By A. C. HARWOOD
The Way of a Child
The Recovery of Man in Childhood (Hodder & Stoughton)

By F. EDMUNDS
Rudolf Steiner's Gift to Education—The Waldorf Schools

Full catalogue available from the publisher.

COMPLETE EDITION

of the works of Rudolf Steiner in the original German. Published by the
Rudolf Steiner Verlag, 4143 Dornach, Switzerland.
General Plan (abbreviated):

A. WRITINGS

I. Works written between the years 1883 and 1925
II. Essays and articles written between 1882 and 1925
III. Letters, drafts, manuscripts, fragments, verses, meditative sayings, inscriptions, etc.

B. LECTURES

I. Public Lectures
II. Lectures to Members of the Anthroposophical Society on general anthroposophical subjects
Lectures to Members on the history of the Anthroposophical Movement and the Anthroposophical Society
III. Lectures and Courses on special branches of work:
Art: Eurythmy, Speech and Drama, Music, Visual Arts, History of Art
Education
Medicine
Science
Sociology and the Threefold Social Order
Lectures given to Workmen at the Goetheanum

The number of lectures amounts to some six thousand, shorthand reports of which are available in the case of the great majority.

C. REPRODUCTIONS and SKETCHES

Paintings, drawings, coloured diagrams, eurythmy forms, etc.

A Complete Bibliographical Survey (with subjects, dates and places where the lectures were given) is available. This, together with all the volumes of the edition, can be obtained from the Rudolf Steiner Bookshops in London, and directly from the *Rudolf Steiner Verlag* (address as above) by the trade.